# GOLD, SILVER AND FREEDOM

## *The Greatest Theft Never Known*

© Alan Dunwiddie

First Edition 2020

---

Copyright Alan Dunwiddie 2020
ISBN 978-87-92295-09-5

Published by AD Publishing, Denmark.

# CONTENTS

# ACKNOWLEDGEMENTS

Writing this book has been a bit like a train journey, so in that vein:-

Thank you to the people still in my carriage in helping with creating this book, listening to the endless theorising, the observations on what might be behind certain events, and giving their input and experiences in return.

Thank you also to those who were there on the journey but are no longer here. I didn't necessarily expect or want you to get off the train, but it happened. Your input has been vital and shines through in many places.

Thank you finally to the internet, the faceless passengers on other carriages and platforms, the ones we will never know or never speak to, but who still travel the same journey through life. Despite the negatives of the internet, it proves there are still individuals out there with a heart, a mind, and the desire to say or write it how they see it, regardless of the possible consequences. The more we share those thoughts and knowledge, the better life can be.

# PREFACE

My childhood was spent growing up in a northern English coal-mining town with relative tranquility then unemployment. Followed by a pretty regular life as an adult during the 1990s, graduating from University, obtaining my first full-time employment, buying a house, meeting a new partner, and then, by the millennium, we had our first child. Work was going well, earnings were rising, and I was saving and investing in all the things we are told to save and invest in for a nice, safe, healthy financial future - Cash savings accounts, Stocks and Shares, pensions and for a while, they all went up nicely. Life was safe, secure, and normal.

Then a series of financial crashes occurred that hammered the supposedly safe portfolio of investments. I didn't set out to invest in technology shares, but in 2000, many got their fingers burnt with a huge crash on the NASDAQ - not only that, but many old economy stocks got dragged down along with them. As things were recovering, along came the World Trade Center in September 2001, and stock markets plummeted. Along with that, so did my savings. In fact, some of the shares were now well below the levels invested in them years before, an early lesson in the financial advice small print - *share prices can go down as well as up.*

Meanwhile, the cash savings accounts didn't quite seem to be keeping up with the prices of goods and services generally, and not keeping up with the increase in house prices at all. How had it all gone wrong? The advice regularly regurgitated in mainstream media had been followed almost to the letter, yet life was now tougher than ever. Especially when in 2002, I found myself unemployed with no income at all and a growing family to feed.

All these things led me to delve into my own alternative research into the world of finance, leading to my first discovery of gold and soon after, silver and their role in representing real money. Of course, I had previously realised the metals could be used to make jewellery and that once upon a time, less enlightened people had used coins made of these metals in their everyday transactions essential to their lives. Luckily, we live in a more enlightened and cleverer financial age, eh?

Maybe not.

In 2006-07, originally as a hobby project, I wrote my first book, imaginatively entitled "How to Invest in Gold and Silver." It was meant just to be a self-published work, distributed to a few friends and relatives, no further than that. However, in late 2007 and early 2008, strange things began to occur in world financial markets again, culminating with the BBC showing footage of people queueing outside Northern Rock, a UK-based bank, patiently waiting their turn to withdraw their savings from the bank in cash. These scenes looked exactly like something being replayed from history, familiar, common even. They were well-documented from a 1907 financial crisis in the USA when the imaginatively-named Knickerbocker Trust got into trouble, and history books tell us decisive action by the financier James Pierpont (J.P.) Morgan saved the day and more commonly-known, the 1930s in the aftermath of the 1929 Wall Street Crash. Only, whereas the BBC was subtly mocking them as fools and playing lots of footage of experts saying they were silly to worry, history showed something written in the book.

"Contrary to Popular opinion, banks do go bust."

— Alan Dunwiddie, 2007

Seeing this occurring geed me up to get focussed on getting the book onto Amazon and other online booksellers. Not even sure if it would sell at all, it was fun to see it out there for public consumption, at least. After the initial excitement, it sold a total of a few thousand copies over the next few years. Not enough to change anyone's life, but a bit of fun, nevertheless. The proceeds were invested into gold, following the premise of the thoughts expressed in the book.

The research and reading have carried on, and a sequel was often considered. There didn't seem to be an endgame or phase switch to justify it, though, and I am glad to have waited because, in March 2020, Corona came along and changed life for most of us worldwide. Not only that, but it's helping to confirm suspicions that the world is a much murkier, dangerous, and sinister place than ever considered when talking about financial manipulations and subtle theft of your hard-earned savings back in 2007. It even brings two of my major interests together - finance and technology.

This book will go over some of the gold and silver basics covered back then, but more so, it attempts to highlight some of the dark incidents that have and are taking place in the world today, concerning money and society. You may be surprised, entertained, and disbelieving. You may get angry with what seems to be really happening, or you may think the author is mad, but hey, isn't that the beauty of free speech and the beauty of the wide range of human emotions we have - a mutual transaction where the author can write this, and the reader can read it and agree or disagree with it? In fact, given the possible endings described in the later chapters, let's be grateful we can still express our differing opinions at all without penalty.

Alan Dunwiddie,
August 2020

# INTRODUCTION

"Gold has at all times been considered the best of testimonies of good faith"

— Rafael Sabatini

People have always wanted and needed to transact with each other. In the beginning, it was barter. The concept of "I'll swap you these fish for some firewood," or such like. While it worked, it was clearly very restrictive and relied on two people needing a direct exchange. What was really needed was a trusted store of value that could be used as payment for goods and services, over and above direct barter. It started with sea-shells and stones that were used as currency, things that could be recognised and counted to account for transactions, moved to commodities like salt, and then ultimately to gold and silver. The English language even has some surviving remnants of this history with 'shell out' as a slang term to pay for something and 'salary' as a monthly payment for work, originating from salt.

Gold (and silver) ultimately became the real units of currency upon which world trade is based. Historically they have replaced all other forms of currency in civilisation because they are durable and not easy to replicate, so future value is relatively assured. Gold is naturally scarce, so perfect as representing value - that ancient alchemy was about trying to turn lead into gold is no coincidence, and the entire gold of the world would fit into a tennis court-sized cube. Gold especially has a reputation for not tarnishing or rusting and is even resistant to some strong acids, meaning that as far as a medium of exchange goes, there is nothing, quite literally, "as good as gold." It's also infinitely divisible in weight as a currency unit, and an ounce of pure gold in the African desert is identical and, therefore, worth exactly the same as an ounce of pure gold in London, making it perfect for international trade.

Gold is, essentially, the perfect item for stored savings and use as a medium of exchange with another party as and when required. You can take a gold coin as payment, bury it in the garden for 2,000 years, and it will remain as shiny, perfect, and representative of its true value as ever. The 2,000 years may seem extreme, yet hoards of this age of gold coins turn up surprisingly often and are worth an awful lot of money. Compare this to if the coins were made of cheaper metal; they'd rust and corrode, often disappearing completely.

It started with exchanging pieces of gold and silver, but that was impractical. Hence, people learnt to melt them down into regular sizes, or weights, then into rounded discs called coins, or 'specie.' Paper money only came into being in the first place as a substitute for the practice of using physical gold and silver in transactions and the trouble of getting your shovel out to bury it then dig it up, perhaps. What happened was that people deposited their gold with a bank, and then the bank would issue them with a promissory note or notes for the value of their gold. People could then use their notes to buy goods, and the person receiving the note knew they now owned the amount of precious metal stated on the note. We'll explore that concept in more detail in **The Beginning of Banking.**

The real problems started occurring when people - normally banks, governments, and forgers, began issuing extra currency backed by the same amount of precious metal, and, in 1971, the last historical link between gold and worldwide currency was removed by the USA, when they removed the link that 1 ounce of gold could be exchanged for 35 dollars and vice-versa. Up to this time, gold had a fixed value in terms of world trade. This will be examined in **Inflation.**

To give you an example of how that paper you have in your wallet, or digital bits on your banking homepage screen have become distended from the real money it once represented, just think of this - A British Pound Sterling was once worth exactly what the words say - *A pound in weight of Sterling silver*. As of the end of August 2020, the same pound of sterling silver is valued at £282, or $376. That is 0.0035% of its original value. How we got to this point is covered in the next few chapters.

It is also worth noting here that gold is a purer representative of true wealth than silver. Although both metals have been heavily used throughout history as currency and to represent wealth, gold has few uses apart from money. In contrast, silver is a heavily used industrial commodity, affecting its price and desirability outside of any investment considerations. For example, back in 2007, some commentators were convinced that the rise of digital photography and the resultant downturn in traditional photography would result in a massive decrease in demand for silver, affecting the price negatively as a result. This may or may not have occurred, as silver did experience some major shifts in price versus fiat currency in

2007-2020. However, silver has many other uses, including electrical components, and such uses are only increasing as technology increases. A factor that will be examined in **Data is the New Oil.**

Possible Government confiscation is also something you might want to consider when choosing your investments, and, as we'll see later, there are many new ways to hold your gold that were simply not possible for ordinary citizens all those years ago in **Into The Future.**

To put the importance of gold in perspective, imagine you time-travelled back to 1910, almost anywhere in the world. The people were transacting with gold and silver, and there was even something called a 'Gold Standard' for international trade. In practice, this meant that gold physically moved between countries according to the balance of trade between those countries. If you had a deficit, you lost gold; if you had a surplus, you gained gold. In other words, a nation-state was just a larger version of how we all run our own household finances. Now, imagine that as part of your time-travelling visit, you tried to pay for something. Having first noted that there was no card terminal for you to tap or even enter your PIN on, no mobile payments, you tried using the modern equivalents of some of the coins in circulation. People may have looked at your legal tender dubiously, noting they were made of steel, nickel, or paper and therefore not worth anything like the coins they were used to - the silver shillings or dollars, the gold sovereigns, all with real intrinsic value. Who was more financially aware, them or us?

In trying to answer that question, this book comprises three parts.

Part 1, which will look at the historic build-up to where we are now. How the wealth of the world ebbs and flows like the tide. Then the journey of the gold and silver since 1910, from the hands of the majority, who were happily using it for their daily transactions then and into the hands of a few today.

Part 2, which will look at the state of the world today and identify some trends underway that, taken to a logical conclusion, are not necessarily good news for the majority either. Freedom is being eroded.

Part 3, which looks at some of the ways it can go in the future and things you can do about it to protect yourself and those you care about.

If you're in any doubt of the value of gold, then just remember that the US government issues each of its pilots with 2 gold sovereigns to use for trade if they are ever shot down in enemy territory. Note that they don't issue them with a huge wad of paper dollars, which probably says something about the worldwide appeal of gold as a tradeable item over even the most well-known internationally accepted national fiat currency.

Much of what is described in Part 2 is conjecture. The future is never guaranteed. However, much of it is an extrapolation of the trends that began just before World War One and continues to this day. Again, you may find you agree in some places and disagree with others. These are the hallmarks of free thought and freedom of expression. Potentially, even those under threat and in danger of being monetized or lost. Enjoy it while you can.

Now, before continuing, look at the performance of gold from around when you took your time travel back and saw the people transacting in real money and now, the period in which we live.

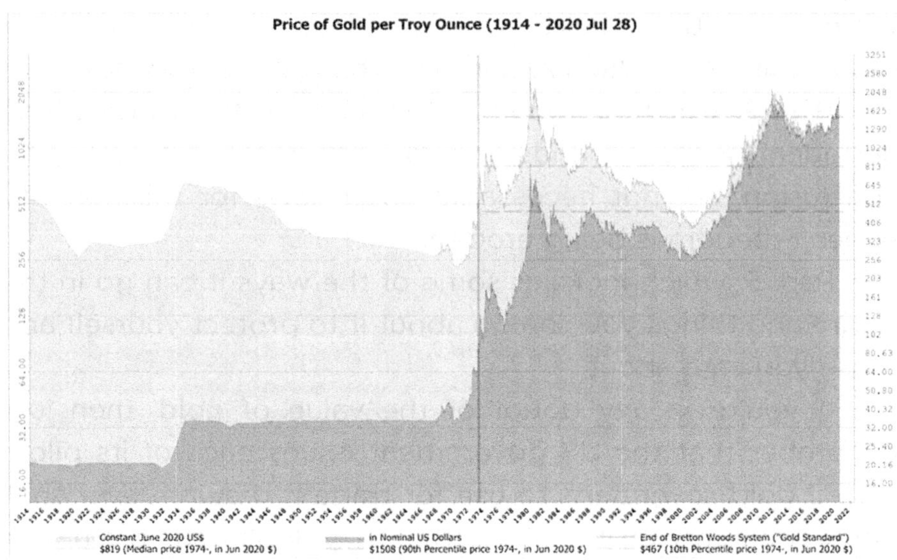


*(Chart of gold price 1914-2020, source: Wikipedia By Codehydro (Alexander Zhikun He) - CC BY-SA 3.0)*

# PART 1

# THE RISE AND FALL OF EMPIRES

"plus ça change, plus c'est la même chose"

— Jean-Baptiste Alphonse Karr, 1849

Or, in less philosophical-sounding English;

"The more it changes, the more it's the same thing."

To explain this further, let's look at the state of the world... An empire rules the world; its capital city was named after one of its greatest leaders. Doric columns and symbols adorn many of the great architectural buildings, demonstrating the power to all who come to gaze upon them and worship the might and achievements of the empire. Just look at all the ornate buildings and imperial symbols everywhere. The locations of past imperial events, the symbols of major victories over imperial enemies. Take their Senate building, for example, where the powerful leaders meet to decide the fate of people throughout the world, and in many cases, who lives and who dies. Or their amphitheatres, where everyone can go to relax, socialise and enjoy seeing their heroes in action. For the poor, there are welfare handouts to ensure they have enough food to eat. The power of this empire (and its capital) was largely the result of a gradual East-West power shift that occurred in the last 100 years, from the former power base and spiritual capital of the empire. The old power base of the empire, still a powerful city in its right, but no longer the world power it once was. It remains a large city inhabited by millions.

What was being described here?

The Roman Empire, with its capital named after the emperor Constantinople, usurping its former capital and spiritual base, Rome itself. It's said that at its imperial peak, Rome had a population of over 2 million, and I'm sure you've seen plenty of photographs of the Colosseum, Parthenon, and Senate to know the architecture being described. Hail Caesar!

Actually no.

The description was of the USA and Washington. Look up the Senate building, along with the courthouses and various other architectural symbols of empire in most towns and cities. You'll see just as many Greek and Roman architectural principles applied as were probably present in Rome, Constantinople, and Carthage at their height. The huge stadiums with football (both types) or baseball, attended by thousands in person and millions via TV - the modern amphitheatres of our time. Then the welfare payments and food stamps doled out to those in need. Now, think how that shift occurred - the sudden shift of the centre of empire from London to Washington, as two world wars, progressed in the last century. Hail Trump!

The only difference seems to be that Rome to Constantinople constituted a West-East shift, whereas London to Washington was an East-West shift. Planet Earth, it seems, is but a clock face, with a pendulum that moves jerkingly, suddenly, and with shock waves to different points on the globe.

So how and why does it happen? It's tempting here to pluck out another phrase, a bit more American and direct - "Follow the Money." What does that mean? Follow the Pounds, Dollars, Euros, Yen, and Yuan? No, they're just currencies - and fiat ones at that, another concept that will be explained later. Follow the money, for there is but one true money, and when you follow it, you realise exactly how and why empires rise and fall. You can't be sure of the timings, but you can learn that something is changing, even if you can't work out when.

In 2020, change feels more inevitable than ever, and the imminent percentage chance seems even greater than back in 2007.

"Study the past, if you would divine the future"

— Confucious

The beginning of a century seems to be an epochal point for the human race on planet earth. Something always seems to happen where the new challengers rise. The nations that are building, expanding, using capital constructively and efficiently to enhance their lives come to challenge the old empire, the one currently dominating. Think of empire as an oak tree; it takes to seed, grows, expands, and becomes strong, each branch expands, each leaf plays its part in absorbing the sunlight, each root spreads to absorb the water. Yet, as the oak grows, the parasites eye it up, and the rot sets in. Sometimes the tree can even look fine from the outside for many years, but inside it is decaying. Empire expands in the same way, then the parasites grow from within, each of them sapping the strength and energy of the once-mighty tree. Meanwhile, new oak trees take root and grow, just as this oak tree once did. Their roots, branches, and leaves spreading to compete with the older, now weakening oak.

As of August 2020, there can be no doubt that the US Empire, or more correctly, if we believe it's merely a power shift from London, the British/Anglo-Saxon Empire is on the wane. Perhaps the future with hindsight will name the Empire more succinctly then we do now? Meanwhile, people look to China as the new imperial challenger, growing massively, using its capital to construct huge cities, factories, and infrastructure to be the new dominant force of the 21st century probably. I am not so sure, as explained later. China will undoubtedly grow, but there are reasons why it may not dominate. What we can be sure of, though, is that the current empire is in decline. The once-efficient branches of the British and American empire are decaying, energy sapped from within, on inefficient schemes. Cost-ineffective projects that are often only created for a few insiders to make money at the expense of everyone else, using up the resources that remain. The current High-speed rail link between London and Birmingham in the United Kingdom, which seems destined to way overrun the estimated 100 billion pound cost and appears to offer little economic benefit to the population as a whole, maybe a prime example. The expensive military incursions in Iraq and Afghanistan, two countries destined to be the death knell of many an empire. The UK got involved both in the 1920s and 1930s, with little success, too, and are classic examples for the United States of America.

Shift back approximately 100 years to 1914. A world war broke out, which ultimately did cross the globe, and many players saw their chance to expand, grabbing resources, territory, and people for future harvesting. For some reason, that war ended without the complete subjugation of the defeated parties in 1918-19. Austria and Hungary were sub-divided, but Germany hardly had any destructive action inside its own borders, bar limited Russian invasion in the East. Perhaps if you lived in Tilsit and the border regions of East Prussia, you might disagree, but the war, for some reason, let Germany off very lightly. Setting the scene for further conflict in 1939-45, where Germany was apparently crushed, with a historic sacking in the style of many an ancient war. Plundering and pillaging on a massive scale, with the subjugation of many of the population through death, rape and displacement. It's said that whereas Americans brought home Lugers, antiques, and artefacts like stamps pillaged from the Reichsmuseums to their families back in the USA, Russians sent home kitchenware, textiles, and furniture they generally knew would improve their family's lot back in mother Russia. Russia even dismantled and shipped entire factories back to the Motherland. Whichever direction it went, East or West, the country was stripped down. What is clear is that in 1945, the USA sat atop the world, with half of the world's gold in its vaults, backing a strong currency and standing as the manufacturing power base for the world, much of which lay in tatters. However, in many ways, who the victors were and who was vanquished isn't so clear when you look beneath the surface.

It seems to be a trait of empires, the imperial hubris of the thinking it'll go on forever. For some reason, US leaders decided immediately after it was over to donate billions to Germany, the defeated foe, to rebuild their country. I'm not quite sure why people would agree on a personal basis to donate billions to someone who just ruined their life for up to 6 years, but it was done in a way that helped people not notice they were silently robbed, another trait of empires. Call it the 'Marshall Aid plan,' and people might not notice, perhaps? Furthermore, impose on the defeated nation that they don't have to contribute militarily to anything internationally - there's a saving of 1% or more of GDP yearly while taking on the benefits of you protecting their oil supplies and trade routes and that 1% can compound over many years into a great investment sum for you to spend on improving your lot. While 1% of GDP doesn't sound like much, it represents a huge chunk of the actual free cash flow of a nation's spending. Just ask British taxpayers, who are seeing their country crumble. At the same time, their then-Prime Minister, David Cameron, committed to a yearly foreign aid budget of 0.7% of UK GDP that remains in statute even today. That some of this has been found to have potentially gone to fund terrorists, pop groups, and other terrible aid projects only add to the pain.

Then there's Japan. Whatever may be said about Donald Trump, he is absolutely right to lament the one-sided trade deal with Japan. For some reason, a load of your elected representatives (if you're in the USA, but whatever country you are in, they are probably undertaking similar schemes and hoping you don't notice), decided back in the late 1940s to gift Japan unfettered access to American markets, while simultaneously granting Japan the right to impose massive protective tariffs on the same types of goods travelling in the opposite direction. No wonder Japan was able to rise from defeated island nation to a huge superpower, where the imperial palace grounds in Tokyo were worth more than the whole of New York by the 1980s.

So, to ask the question again, who won World War 2? On paper, the Allies, primarily the USA and UK, did. Russia apparently did too, but in their case, a particularly pyrrhic victory that statistically has been suggested to mean 100 million fewer people are living in Russia today than would otherwise have been, had World War 2 and the Stalinist purges not happened. In reality, what happened next was that the victors then began a decline. In the case of once-Great Britain, a huge decline with the loss of the resource-rich colonies to ending the 1970s on a near-GDP per capita par with Albania. In the case of the USA, less apparent, but still true, nevertheless. It becomes more apparent with the USA when certain other factors are examined later, namely Bretton Woods and the end of gold convertibility in 1971.

Britain's fall from Victorian greatness and the world number 1 spot is a classic gold case story in itself. Beginning 1900 atop the world, it got involved in a rather expensive war in South Africa that marked the beginning of the end. Instead of being the typical Victorian war by British standards, where it was over rather quickly and costlessly for an immense amount of return - Think Zanzibar in 1896, for example, where the "war" with Britain lasted all of 38 minutes, this one took much longer to accomplish. Those pesky Boers in the Transvaal and Orange Free State decided to put up a fight of it, and it turned into an embarrassing and costly 3 year-long victory for Britain, to say nothing of the horrors for the Boers themselves, many of whom died not on the battlefield but were women and children in concentration camps. Yes, when an empire is on the wane, human rights, personal freedoms, and common decency are also among the casualties. What's not often mentioned in this is that the Boer War was, in fact, a battle to grab resources - the gold and diamonds being two major ones. Even today, South Africa remains a top 10 gold-producing nation and has the world's deepest gold mine - Tautona, Carletonville, at 3,900 metres or 2.4 miles underground. There really are few depths man won't go to for gold and that this mine is in former Boer territory is also a clue. You could even argue that the Boer War was a classic example of a nation-state being utilised by outside forces beyond the people it purports to represent, to get what those outside forces want. Cecil Rhodes, the man behind De Beers diamond company, has had plenty written about him, which only barely scratches the surface - The Rhodes scholarship and Council for Foreign Relations are two of his legacies that even today have a huge influence on world events and the future for us all. The common people of the UK, who sent the men to fight that war and for whom the names on war memorials hint at hidden tales of sadness and destroyed lives, certainly didn't get rich off it. It's also interesting the UK media slant on the war that the fight was for something worthwhile, and the Boers were demonised at the time by the media. Much the same as you get when watching or reading about Russia, Syria, Iraq, Iran, *<insert name of next target country here>* in the modern era. Even today, if you happen to live in the UK in one of many of the Victorian and Edwardian terraces with such names as Milner, Mafeking, Buller, or Kimberley, you are living in a 120-year-old propaganda item, for these are the names of major characters or battles from the time.

World War 1 was the big struggle that broke the British Imperial camel's back, so to say. In return for massive losses, both human and economic - all it got were a few extra territories to add to the empire, mostly in Africa, off the defeated new challenger, Germany. For sure, there were also some major oil fields in Iran and Iraq now ripe for exploitation, but the country itself didn't seem to benefit much from them, mainly private corporations. A trend that has ballooned as the twentieth century has progressed. The overspend and debt from that conflict fed into 1920s hardships, the gradual replacement of gold sovereigns and half-sovereigns with banknotes representing the same face value but being yet another example of state-authorised clipping of the coinage. In 1926, the UK finally closed the gold convertibility window, where you could convert your banknotes into the gold equivalent. Apparently, the stock market actually rose that day, despite governmental worries it would collapse. Those in the know had already realised the last thing you'd want to be holding now was paper pounds instead of gold ones, and in

1931, the UK suffered a major devaluation of the British Pound as the market caught up with reality.

Zoom through history back almost 100 years again to 1815. The defeated imperial superpower of France hands the imperial baton to Great Britain and London. It may not have necessarily seemed obvious when Waterloo concluded the Napoleonic wars once and for all that was going to happen, but France was bled dry. Huge losses in manpower and redirection of resources from productive purposes for the good of people to the production of arms to fight a war ultimately lost. Skip forward briefly 36 years to 1851, and the Great Exhibition at the Crystal Palace in London is telling you exactly where the money and power have migrated to.

Let's hop in the Tardis once more and travel back to 1713 and the treaty of Utrecht. Ostensibly a peace treaty, but one that sees the decline of Spain and the handing of the baton to France. Spain loses the Netherlands and is crippled by wars, internal and external, beginning a huge international decline that sees it lose the valuable colonies in South America, the Philippines, and Cuba. Even if that last part took a lot longer - it was the 1890s before one of the new challengers, the USA decided to flex its muscles and go on a land and resource grab at Spain's expense. As a case study of where empire goes ultimately, even 300 years later, Spain has never really recovered to any decent level. Certainly, it's not as poor now, but even in the 1930s, it had a large civil war, and in the 1980s, it was a dictatorship under Franco. That democracy and freedom decline as an empire declines seem to be a fact of life and death.

Of course, during the 1600s, Spain was the dominant power in Europe, and that really is no surprise. Failure to invade England with the defeat of the Spanish Armada in 1588 was irrelevant in reality, once it conquered lands in the Americas, bringing with it massive resources and imperial tons (or metric tonnes) of gold and silver. Did the 1500s belong to South America? Who knows, there were certainly great empires there that are lost to our history books, and they may well have had most of the gold in that period. Advanced civilisations that knew a lot more than the Europeans did about many things. It was probably luck, in many ways, that Spain managed to conquer so much of South America. Depending on who you read, it's suggested that the diseases brought by the Europeans are what really aided that victory. Diseases that travelled quicker than the Europeans themselves and perhaps killed up to 97% of the population, much of it in areas that the Europeans hadn't even reached yet. There are fascinating journals telling of early journeys by European explorers up an Amazon River teeming with life and trade, yet, 50 years later, journals tell of journeys up a deserted Amazon devoid of human life.

To travel back further in history, the early medieval period probably belonged to China. For this insight, just read Marco Polo's "The Travels." Medieval China, ruled by Kublai Khan, a descendant of Genghis, was a rich place.

> "In Xanadu did Kubla Khan
> A stately pleasure dome decree:
> Where Alph, the sacred river, ran
> Through caverns measureless to man
> Down to a sunless sea.
> So twice five miles of fertile ground
> With walls and towers were girdled round:
> And there were gardens bright with sinuous rills,
> Where blossomed many an incense-bearing tree;
> And here were forests ancient as the hills,
> Enfolding sunny spots of greenery."
>
> *Or a Vision in a Dream. A Fragment*
> *- Samuel Taylor Colleridge*

Perhaps Colleridge's poem was inspired by Marco Polo marvelling at rich Chinese cities of immense scale. If to be believed, it states city walls 5 miles long each side on Xanadu (modern-day Chengdu) alone. Huge, varied trade was taking place, busy people involved in a whole host of economic activities, where stories tell of huge Chinese boats plying the rivers and seas on a scale unknown to Europeans even hundreds of years later. *The Travels* tells of cities with, if Polo is accurate, populations of a million or more and that there are many of these cities, with riches beyond his comprehension. Polo also gives us an ultimate clue to the richness of this empire - for he marvels at something else unknown to Europeans - the Chinese don't use gold and silver coinage like in Europe; they use paper, the bark of the mulberry tree is used as the currency on which trade is based. While marvelling upon this great empire, with millions of subjects and riches beyond imagination, we should begin to think a little on another question, one largely undocumented. Where and why did it all go wrong? What happened between Polo's travels and the China that became a sleepy backward backwater in world trade and politics for hundreds of years and only now is re-emerging? That should be a great clue because it's exactly where we are today and where gold and silver come into the equation. What Polo marvels at also is the trust the people have in the great Kublai Khan at Xanadu, who benevolently looks after all the gold on behalf of the people, who at any time could pop along to his vault and exchange those paper promises for the equivalent value in gold. Centralisation, trust, and government...this whole story will later begin to sound familiar.

"History never repeats, but it rhymes."

— Mark Twain, (possibly)

Before the medieval times, who knows, there were many great rich cities along the Silk Road that are now just ruined, with little left of their tales of immense wealth. Merv in Iran, for example, had perhaps 500,000 people there at its peak, was a major centre of learning, and is now just a raised shell in a desert. The point is, people and wealth move, civilisation and empire grows, lives, and dies. It is never fixed, and it definitely never stays the same forever.

As an empire grows, it gains wealth, then freedom, culture, and choice flourish. As it declines, wealth is lost, freedom dies, and censorship normally rises. Follow the gold, and you begin to understand why.

# THE BEGINNING OF BANKING

"If you want to rob a bank get a gun; if you want to rob a country, get a bank."

— Anon

Medieval Europeans didn't have that trust in centralised systems then that the Chinese did but fast forward in time to the twentieth and early twenty-first century, and they definitely do. It moves in phases, just like that pendulum described earlier. During Greek and Roman times, the coins started out as pure gold and silver, but someone is always looking to make a profit from it, and they often work out a way to do so. It probably started in ancient Greece, the first time someone realised they could file a tiny amount off the edge of a gold coin, then once enough filings were accumulated, melt it down and press a new coin. The answer to that crime? To print raised dotted bumps on the edges of coinage, a practise that continues to this day, with the original reason lost in time. The other answer was the death penalty for anyone found guilty of "clipping the coinage." Back then, they realised the consequences of the death of trust and trade if people could not trust the coinage itself as a medium of exchange.

It was only a matter of time before governments then thought up their own inventive ways to "clip the coinage" and make them legally enforceable. During times of war, funds were desperately needed to buy weapons, pay armies, and fund campaigns, which often led to recalls of the coinage. The people would hand over their gold and silver trustingly, then new coins would be issued with the same nominal value, but weighing less in terms of gold and silver. The government could then melt down extra coins with the leftover metal and hey presto - a victimless crime where creditors could be paid... except you've just inflated the number of currency units in circulation and the economy will adjust to reflect that. It may take some time, but it almost undoubtedly will eventually.

To demonstrate how far this went, we can further look at ancient Rome and the decline. The empire started out with coins of pure gold, but over the years, decades and centuries, the coins shrank in size. In the latter years of the empire, coins of copper, silver, and gold started being mixed with other metals and then replaced. You can, of course, guess the ultimate effect on prices and trust in the economy. Even though it's not documented, we can probably guess it was the first instance of *Gresham's Law*.

Gresham's law is simply that bad money forces out good. What this means in practice is that if you have 2 equal denomination items, say a £1 paper banknote and a £1 gold sovereign, which would you spend first? Then, which would you hold onto if it was apparent that the value of the metal comprising that coin was worth more than £1? It's exactly what happened in the USA in the 1960s, as inflation took hold, and people realised that nickels and dimes were worth more in silver content than the nominal 5 and 10 cent value stamped on them. There are even stories of some enterprising people going to the bank and withdrawing money in coins, or visiting the mint to exchange their paper dollars for wheelbarrow-sized piles of the coins themselves. Many of these would be melted down later and never re-enter the market as coinage. It should make you think that the next time the government talks about a "shortage of coins in circulation," that they may have caused it themselves through inflating the amount of money in circulation. The UK had until recently a situation where the 1p and 2p copper coins, the 1971 versions, contained more copper value than the nominal value upon them. Whether you want to hoard thousands of them is up to you. Even if you don't have space, it's a funny thought to think these are the coins closest to representing intrinsic value in the UK. Going back further in time, we can guess those Romans felt the same way, perhaps not the first few times, but an increasing number probably realised with each inflationary round that they best hoard the good coins and spend the bad ones. It probably goes some way to explaining the immense amount of Roman coin hoards found across the territories of the empire. Bad times came; what we don't know is why the people never made it back to dig them up and reclaim them. There must be some fascinating untold stories out there.

As an interesting side note, as a child in the 70s-80s, I became interested in numismatism, the collecting of coins. Of the pre-decimal shillings which were still then in circulation representing the decimal era 5p, the pre-1947 shillings actually contained some silver and were thus worth more than the nominal 5p value upon them. Imagine the joy, after checking the date of every coin received to actually find once or twice, a George VI pre-1947 shilling. Little was it realised then, but Gresham's Law was being followed, and they're still in a tin somewhere. Not only was the government actively debasing/clipping the coinage back then too, but 1947 should also be another clue as to the reasons why it happens. World War 2 ended in 1945, leaving the UK financially crippled and with massive debts to repay. It sounds like the perfect time to copy the Romans, issue coins made of cheaper metal, and then stamp the same nominal value on them.

Taking the lead from Polo's stories of China, modern banking began in Italy, in Florence, in medieval times. Up to that point, people trusted the value of the coins being in the metal itself. They probably became adept when accepting coins as payment, at running a finger along the edge to check all the raised dots were present, and thus, the coin was unclipped and worth accepting. What the enterprising bankers of Florence realised was that they could become deposit keepers for the merchants. So, rather than large amounts of gold changing hands constantly and requiring to be rechecked with every transaction for possible fraud, they could offer to hold the gold in permanent safe storage for the merchants and issue promissory notes against it. The merchants could pass these promissory notes between themselves, safe for the amount of gold and silver stated on them. Instead of the costs of gold checking and transport, the merchants would then pay the banks a fee for the storage.

The system sounds all good so far, as long as you can trust the parties and counterparties. A key part of that is, of course, to know that the note can be redeemed for the amount of metal/specie stated on it *immediately*. A banker will build up his reputation to ensure that promise is kept. You'll have noticed by now that we are now one step removed from physical ownership of the metals themselves. Later, you'll see that trust isn't necessarily a guaranteed thing.

The next part of the story is that the banks looked at all this gold sitting in their vaults and thought to themselves, how can we increase our profits on this? Now, there are perfectly legal ways to do this, and some not so ethical or legal. One legal way is to lend out the gold of a merchant to other merchants to conduct more profitable dealings. This should not be done without the permission of the merchant/depositor. What the bank might do is say to depositor A, I can pay you 4% on your gold by lending it to merchant B. The bank then lends it to merchant B, on certain repayment terms, at say, 5% interest, and thus the bank pockets 1% for their role in brokering the transaction. There's nothing wrong with this - the gold still ultimately belongs to one person and exists once in the accounting transaction.

The key point of sound money is that money can only exist once in any given period. As soon as you manage to make it exist multiple times in a single period, the concept of sound money has been eroded.

Where it starts to get contrived is if the banker lends out the gold in his vault without asking merchant A if he agrees. The bank, for example, might have worked out that 95% of the gold in the vault never, ever leaves the vault. Who would ever know if he loaned a small portion, say 5%, of it out and pocketed the whole 5% interest profit for himself instead of sharing the proceeds with the people whose gold he is lending? Well, the depositors would know if all of them turned up the same day with their promissory notes to get their gold redeemed. The last 5% of them would find, as did *Old Mother Hubbard*, that when she got there, the cupboard was bare. However, you are likely to get away with it for years without being noticed.

You may well have worked out that lending your savings out without your permission as a bank depositor amounts to nothing more than theft. Yet, these are the exact tricks that were perpetrated against the people years ago, and now it's got even worse because, in more modern times, it was found that less than 10% of the gold ever left the vault, leading to the legalisation of the next major theft, *Fractional Reserve Banking.*

# FRACTIONAL RESERVE BANKING

"By this means (fractional reserve banking) government may secretly and unobserved, confiscate the wealth of the people, and not one man in a million will detect the theft."

— John Maynard Keynes

Once the banks had worked out that statistically only a small percentage of the gold ever left their vaults, they could start to get cleverer about making money out of the deposited savings. In a method called *fractional reserve banking*, which sounds mathematical and possibly deliberately opaque, a common theme of financial sleight-of-hand. In reality, it means an increased number of currency units in circulation at any one time against the same amount of gold in the vault. Simply put, banks could issue new money to circulate alongside the existing.

This means that subject to certain requirements, a lending bank can create money out of thin air when loaning money. It is a popular misconception, persisting to the modern-day, that there has to be an equivalent 1:1 deposit in the bank made by someone else. Under this system of fractional reserve banking, a bank can create loans for multiples of the deposits it holds. It does this by treating its reserves - the money it holds, including the money deposited by customers - as a fraction of what it is allowed to lend.

For example, consider a scenario where a bank has a reserve requirement of 10%. Not unrealistic in 2020. If you deposit £1,000 with a bank, the bank is ultimately allowed to loan out £9,000 to potential borrowers. This means that there is an extra £9,000 circulating in the economy and that while you thought you were rich with your hard-earned £1,000, there are now other people with spending power too, all thanks to you. The only difference being that the bank loaned them theirs against assumed future earnings and added interest for them to repay in the future too.

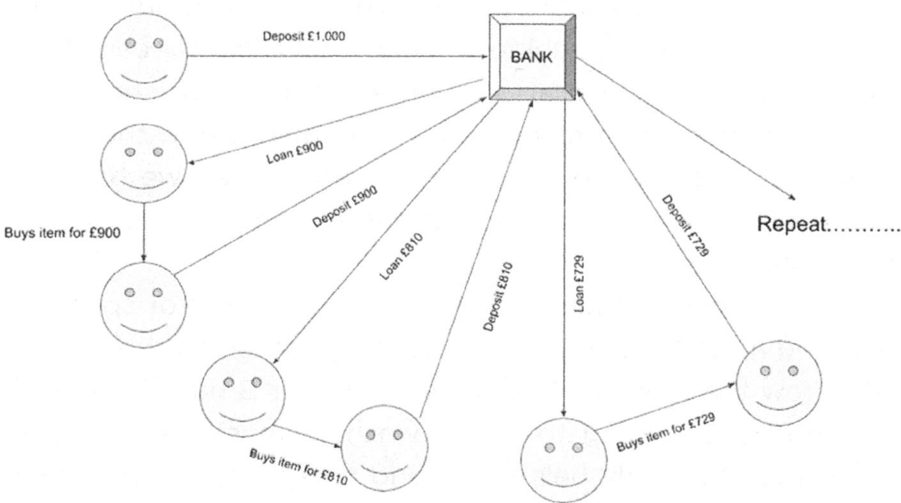


This is due to the cycle whereby borrowers spend their money on goods and services, and the people receiving the money then deposit their new wealth in turn at a bank, who can then create even more 90% loans against these new deposits. Now your original £1,000 deposit is being gradually diluted, and it's spending power devalued by newly created currency.

Not only that, but this has become enshrined in law as the reserve lending requirement. Yes, governments worldwide all have in law that banks can carry out this practice. At the time of writing, the UK reserve lending requirement is 10%.

To put this in perspective, most of us are trained to accept that banks pay lower interest in savings and charge higher interest on loans, the difference being their profit margin. That is only true if the earlier example is followed, where the bank agrees with the depositor to lend their savings out for an agreed period, say 5 years, and then loan it out for the same agreed amount of time to the borrower. In banking, that is called a time deposit.

However, modern fractional reserve banking usually includes all deposits, even current/checking accounts, in their reserve requirement. In the above example, the original depositor may have only decided to deposit the money to buy, say, a new washing machine when a great offer appears. If the other depositors have also put their money into short-term accounts, there is nothing to stop everyone from withdrawing their money at or around the same time. Then we have the basic law of money broken - the same money exists twice at the same time.

It gets worse. Imagine if the original depositor spots the washing machine of their dreams and pops off to the bank to withdraw the money. Meanwhile, borrower B has also loaned the money intending to buy a washing machine and spots the same offer, only he's ready and nips in and buys it. Now depositor A, who started the chain, has been undercut by someone else using his savings!

It breaks several rules of real money:-

- It doesn't get a prior agreement of the depositor to lend out their money.

- It doesn't lend against allocated accounts, like time deposits, where the original money deposited is tied up and therefore 'lost' for the period of the loan.

- It allows the same money to exist multiple times at the same time.

Fractional reserve banking certainly improves the profitability of banks. Say you get 5% interest on your savings - an extreme figure for 2020, but historically reasonable, and the bank loans money out at 10%. Using the example above, that's a total of £9000 they have loaned out, earning 10% interest on every loan. Meanwhile, there's £10,000 deposited in total that only needs 5% paid on it. The adding of interest subject is covered in **Usury.**

Fractional Reserve Banking got a large mention in the 1947 film, "It's a Wonderful Life." In the film, worried depositors are seen turning up at the local private bank in a panic to withdraw their money. They also turn up to the small Savings and Loan institution run by James Stewart and try to withdraw their money. He makes an impassioned speech explaining that their savings are loaned out to other members of his institution, reminding them that the private bank is not so generous or fair. Customers are unaware of behind the scenes machinations, where the large private bank is trying to put him out of business. He eventually backs up trust in the business with his own money and manages to survive. There are clear messages in this film, also regarding **Usury**, large corporations, and community. All covered in subsequent chapters. The USA had suffered many bank runs in the 1930s, as worried depositors took out their dollars to pay for emergencies, or just to retain them as physical savings in their house. It's estimated that by 1933, 9,000 banks had collapsed, so there's no doubt this film would've meant a lot more to that generation watching it than us today. When it was released, the film was regarded suspiciously by the authorities, even as communist and subversive. It's still as relevant, though, and well worth watching at least this clip.

The 1964 Disney film "Mary Poppins", starring Julie Andrews and Dick van Dyke, also demonstrates how a run on a fractional reserve bank works. In one scene, the bank manager sings about funding imperial projects like 'railways in Africa' and 'dams in Egypt.' The bank then snatches tuppence from a young boy who then shouts, "Give me money back!" This prompts other bank customers to be concerned about why the bank manager won't give his money back, and they begin demanding theirs, too, leading to the bank closing the withdrawal counters. With the withdrawal counters closed, the bank accidentally spills a huge pile of gold coins on the floor, a subtle suggestion, perhaps, to help you realise they do have your money really. As long as all depositors don't want their money back simultaneously, banks are fine. Trust is key.

Fractional Reserve Banking is also responsible for something we all nowadays take as a positive thing because it means we get a day off work. *Bank Holidays*. The origin of bank holidays is historically based on banks taking a holiday from paying out to customers. They could tally the books during this holiday and ensure that they weren't technically insolvent from having lent out too much money against deposits. The idea is that, if the bank was insolvent, they could call in a few favours during the day off and be in a position to continue the business, as usual, the next day of opening. If it sounds like something ancient, think again. The whole USA even had an eight-day bank holiday in 1933, after an emergency law was passed to stop more banks from going bust.

As to Fractional Reserve Banking itself, well, it gets worse. In 2020 during the Corona crisis, the USA simply reduced the reserve lending requirement to zero, giving banks the power to issue new money with interest added, without any savings in the bank to back it up. This is further described in **The Crown**. The media response in reporting this incredible, never-seen-before, financial act?

Zilch.

# FIAT CURRENCY

"The problem with fiat money is that it rewards the minority that can handle money, but fools the generation that has worked and saved money."

— Adam Smith

Up to now, you may have noticed that money has been a matter for private citizens to manage, and they have the right to choose whether they wish to transact with a bank or hold onto their wealth themselves. They also have the right to decide what to transact in and when. This point is highlighted in fascinating stories about the Caribbean islands in the 1600s, where currencies from all the major countries - France, Britain, and Spain, would openly circulate together and be exchanged. The key point is that people knew the weights of the coins to conduct business properly. 'Pieces of Eight' were no more than situations where people had taken a larger coin and subdivided it into 8 pieces to complete a transaction. At this point, government interference in the process was minimal to non-existent.

Then something changed.

Countries began to take control of the nation's finances, introducing laws and gradually shepherding all the private banks and gold under their single control. Then, ultimately, they had the sole power of issuance of currency. That in itself is bad enough since now they could dilute the wealth of those already holding promissory notes against the gold in the vault, but the next step was to enforce usage of the national currency in all transactions. This is what a fiat currency is, a currency by a decree. You're basically telling those enterprising traders and pirates in the Caribbean that you may no longer use French Francs or Spanish Doubloons; for example, you must use British Pounds and only British Pounds. They may not listen for a while, but customs officials and the military can be useful tools in helping enforce it eventually.

And with that, you can almost hear the click of a prison cell door closing on financial freedom.

Being able to create and manage a currency is indeed a powerful thing. By now, you hopefully understand the difference between currency by governmental decree and hard currency. You may or may not also have realised that, in reality, gold, as the world's oldest currency, is the item of constant value, and it is national currencies that decline or fall in value compared to the price of gold. When you start looking at things this way, you begin to realise that when commentators talk about "the price of gold," this is a misnomer, and perhaps a truer title would be "the value of the national currency" or such like.

The average life of a fiat currency is 27 years, according to a survey of 775 fiat currencies by Dollardaze.org. The British Pound has existed since 1694 and wins some kind of record for lasting so long. However, to put that in perspective, remember it no longer represents a pound of sterling silver and measured that way, has lost 99.996% of its 1694 value.

"Give me control of a nation's money, and I care not who makes the laws."

— Amschel Rothschild

If you doubt the power of control of a nation's money, then the words of a Rothschild help put it into context. After all, during the Nineteenth century, the family was said to have amassed the largest personal fortune in the world. Now, let's look at an example where someone attempted to issue their own alternative currency. We don't even need to go back very far in history - just about ten years in fact. Also, not to some third world country, but the United States of America and examine the case of the *Liberty Dollar*.

## LIBERTY DOLLAR

Bernard Von Nothaus was responsible for setting up a new private currency called "Liberty Dollar". Liberty dollars were available either as certificates, with the precious metal held in a vault or as actual minted coins, with genuine silver content. They were available online and mentioned in the original publication of "How to Invest in Gold and Silver" in 2007. Gaining only a brief mention as they did not seem to represent a globally accessible way of obtaining metals and were very US-focussed. However, there did seem to be value for US residents in them, and if they had gained traction, perhaps they could have become a rival currency. Sadly, the US government didn't allow this to happen; instead, they seized the assets and took them to court. Court documents revealed during the case mentioned there were 250,000 holders of Liberty dollar certificates, so it really had become quite popular. His crime for which he spent several years in prison? "Making coins resembling and similar to United States coins."

In late 2014, after about 7 years, a federal judge ordered that all coins be returned to their original owners. In reality, was Liberty Dollar cheating anyone? The Liberty Dollar contained the same silver content as a silver US dollar from 100 years ago; the margin of profit was clearly stated to buyers, as was the fact that it was a modern minted coin.

The key lesson from this cautionary tale should not be lost on anyone. Those controlling the nation's money don't like competition.

## CURRENCY DELIVERY

Now you have control of a single currency that you have decreed everyone must use; you also have control of the tap where it can be turned on and off.

It's worth considering how our currency and methods of payment have physically changed en route to the present day, as there have been 3 major steps or eras. While the dates are approximate, it's a fascinating one to think about, especially the march in the last twenty or so years towards digital fiat currency:-

Up to 1914

The circulation of coinage representing and containing the wealth by being made of gold, silver, and even copper for the lowest denominations. You are responsible for the mint of new coins and the exchange and melting down of damaged or worn coins, but once they are in circulation, that's it. A lesser bank branch network is required here. You issue promissory notes for larger denominations, for international trade, for example, but most people don't even have bank accounts.

1914 to 1990s

The circulation of metal coinage and banknotes representing the wealth, but not containing the wealth. The sleight-of-hand is well underway now, as the physical wealth, the gold and silver, is being, or has been prised from the hands, pockets, and tins of the people. The initial promise being that the people can always exchange these new representations for the real thing they handed over at your vault. This carries a little more responsibility since, as a fiat currency issuer, you must manufacture the coinage and notes and physically deliver them to people to transact with. That's when an agency of money distribution branches becomes necessary. E.g., bank branches, post offices, and more latterly, ATMs. People may begin to smell a rat if even the substitute tokens aren't there to transact with when they need them.

1990s - Present day

The circulation of digital money to everyone via bank accounts, so a bank account becomes a necessity now. This digital money has never previously existed as physical coinage or banknotes, and most certainly doesn't represent any gold or silver. It's also extremely easy to distribute - a few computer screen presses may even be enough. No mint or printing press is required, no distribution network of bank and post office branches, creating and distribution can be fairly instant.

If you are old enough, you may recall that some people were unhappy about the switch from physical currency to digital in the 1990s. It can help nudge the public along the path to acceptance when the media also posts a few stories around this time, pointing out the amount of untaxed economic activity by people insisting on transacting in physical cash.

This era also implies a much-decreased role for banks at a local level, as they no longer have much of a role in delivering money to customers. Many customers don't need it at all, and those that do often just use an ATM. When you think about the diminished need for physical currency distribution in population centres, it's no surprise that bank branches and post offices have closed in such great numbers in the last 20 years.

Obviously, there is some overlap between the eras. Gold and silver coins are still produced even today, but mostly for collectors only. Banknotes and coins from the second era also existed at some points in the first era and are still produced, but in much lower volumes since the internet took over.

# USURY

"Money was intended to be used in exchange, but not to increase at interest. And this term interest, which means the birth of money from money, is applied to the breeding of money because the offspring resembles the parent. Wherefore of all modes of getting wealth, this is the most unnatural."

— Aristotle

The last two chapters began to talk about a new concept invented by enterprising bankers, hundreds, perhaps thousands of years ago - the lending out of stored savings in the vault to other parties, with interest added to cover the risk and make a profit for the person lending their savings out. This is called *Usury*.

Or is it? Up until the medieval era, *Usury* meant lending money with interest. During the medieval era, it was split into two meanings:-

*Lending with Interest* - the acceptable face of loaning money out

*Usury* - Lending with unfair or excessive terms

Without fractional reserve banking, lending money can actually be fine. It involves three parties:-

- The *lender*, who is willing to take the risk of lending his money to someone else in return for a profit. He must accept that for the duration of the loan, his original deposit is gone, but he gets it back later.

- The *broker*, who takes a percentage of the interest rate

- The *borrower*, who wishes to use the money for their own life requirements or a profitable enterprise that will pay them in extra money as profit

This transaction is perfectly compatible with true money. The lender is willing to lose his money if the borrower defaults on repayment. The money will then belong to who the borrower passed it onto.

The problem is when fractional reserve banking is involved.

For when you realise that fractional reserve banking is nothing more than the creation of new money, with interest added, then this is where the major theft occurs.

Going back to **Fractional Reserve Banking**. A fractional reserve ratio of 10% meant your £1,000 of savings deposit ultimately allowed the bank to create new loans of £9,000 to other customers. That's not the end of the story, because the bank also stipulates, say, an interest rate of 10%, to be paid by those customers. In other words, those customers actually need to find more money than the original £9,000 they borrowed to pay back. Yes, there is now £10,000 in circulation, but the amount of money owed to the bank is now £9,000 + the interest due.

Throughout the loan, the total repayment might be £10,000 extra in interest. So cash of £10,000 in the economy is now supporting a created debt requirement of £19,000.

This puts people on a very competitive footing with each other. They all need to compete to earn plenty from the £10,000 pool, just to repay their loans and the new interest. Obviously, it doesn't all need to be repaid all at once, but there simply isn't enough money in circulation compared to what's ultimately due in debt. Worse, on the ledger, the banks can add the yearly interest profit to their own account and create extra loans on that too! In the long term, unless more money enters the economy, someone will default on their loan repayments.

Now you maybe understand the true power of banks being able to create extra money out of the same stored savings. It's not just about the new money entering the economy, but the creation of interest to be paid to them too. Their risk on the loan is small because they can create 9 loans for every customer deposit and get interest on every one above what they may be paying as savings interest. Banking is indeed a very profitable business. Especially when, as you'll read later, you manage to remove one of the major risks from the equation - that every depositor can turn up at once and demand their gold back.

It also explains why governments, individuals, and many businesses are heavily in debt. There simply isn't enough money in the system to repay it all. The debt itself is unpayable - especially when you look at the size of national debts. They can never be repaid, and expecting us all to continue paying the interest on these manufactured loans ensures perpetual debt slavery. Especially loans the citizens themselves didn't even agree to take out.

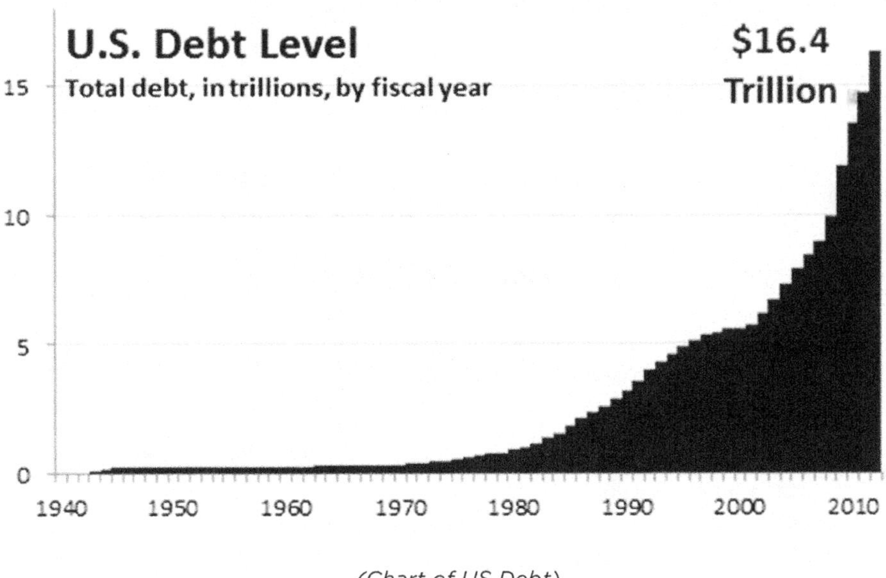



*(Chart of US Debt)*

Now, going back to the medieval definitions. Does all this sound like *lending at interest*, or *usury*, in your opinion?

Given the brevity of that thought, it can be little surprise that history brings up so many philosophers and financial experts commenting on the system of usury. Like Aristotle, right at the beginning. Let's not also forget two of the biggest historical opponents of usury were Jesus Christ and The Prophet Mohammed. Islam forbids it completely, and The Bible has many anti-usury references. As many of the Islamic countries still also prefer to save in gold, it may well be possible there's a shared psychological scar from some financial crisis in the region, long-forgotten and lost to history.

# INFLATION

> "It is well enough that people of the nation do not understand our banking and monetary system, for if they did, I believe there would be a revolution before tomorrow morning."
>
> — Henry Ford

It seems to be that every great nation in history begins with good intentions or promises of a strong currency. Before the USA, Britain removed its link to gold in the 1920s, after its own inflation problems due to the costs of paying for World War 1.

In the prior chapters, we looked at private enterprise methods of extra currency unit creation, via clipping the coinage and the banking system, leading up to government assuming the role of managing national currencies. Giving a single National bank the power or privilege of running a national fiat currency has led to many new methods of inflating the currency. Worse still, history is a phenomenal guide to how common it is, yet mankind never seems to have learnt, or constantly forgets the lesson. In the rest of this chapter, we'll look at how the USA did it, but whatever country you live in right now, you transact with and are paid in fiat currency, with the same practices occurring behind the smoke and mirrors.

As the current empire, the USA began 1900 with a strong, growing country, an economic powerhouse destined to lead the world, and best of all, their currency was all denominated in gold and silver.

The USA removed its link in gradual phases, but three major milestones stand out in history:-

- The creation of the Federal Reserve, in 1913, just before World War One, handing control of the US national currency to private banking interests. To emphasise the importance of this, do you remember Amschel Rothschild's quote from earlier? James Corbett's superb "Century of Enslavement - History of the Federal Reserve" video and podcast documentary is highly recommended for the full history of how that happened.

- 1933 at the height of the US depression. At this time, an ounce of gold was exchangeable for $20 by government decree. Still, the government made ownership of gold illegal for US citizens and ordered the forcible confiscation of all privately held gold. Afterward, gold was revalued to $35 an ounce, although it remained illegal for a US citizen to own gold right up until the 1970s. As you can probably see if, as a US citizen, you held gold at this time, you just got robbed of $15 for each ounce you originally held! The other side of the equation was that there were suddenly 75% more dollars in circulation, backed by the same underlying amount of gold. The extra currency units in circulation are a classic example of debasing the coinage and Inflation.

- While the owning of gold was illegal for US citizens, the USA sat atop international trade after World War 2, allowing gold convertibility at the same price of 35 dollars an ounce for other nations. This was called the 'Bretton Woods' agreement, referring to the location where it was signed. However, partly due to the cost of paying for the Vietnam War, the number of dollars in circulation began rising in the 1950s and 1960s. Nations like France and West Germany seized their chance to exchange their devaluing dollars for the real thing, gold at $35 an ounce. In 1971, the window for exchanging gold was officially closed.

During the 1960s, before removing the gold peg, the USA had built up to this by also removing from circulation all lower priced silver coinage, such as dimes and nickels, and minting new, cheaper alloy versions with the same face value.

Coincidentally - if there is such a thing as coincidence, with no national currency officially tied to any store of value, the 1970s then saw rampant inflation, with gold finally reaching an all-time high of $850 per ounce in 1980 and silver peaking at $49 in 1980 after beginning the decade at under $2. Yes, you read that right, a 20-times plus return for holding what is probably the world's safest stores of value in your pocket. Could such times be repeated? Well, tie in today's current period of government-reported low inflation figures and indifference amongst a general population that has forgotten that gold and silver used to be the coins in our pockets, to the costs of wars in Afghanistan, Iraq, and Libya and as of 2020, the massive costs of the Corona crisis, which are examined in **The Crown**.

Sounds eerily similar, and therefore you might want to exchange some of your paper money "backed by the full faith of the Government" for some gold, just in case. It cannot be guaranteed that your gold investments will increase 20-fold in terms of your local currency. Still, it is guaranteed, barring theft (governmental or otherwise) or such like that your ounce of gold will still be worth an ounce of gold, less any fees, when you choose to cash it in, and that it will still be tradable for an ounce of gold worth of goods such as food and clothing. This applies even if the Government goes bankrupt and the Dollar, Pound, or Euro ever become worthless. For whereas a government can create as much currency as it likes, the amount of gold and silver can only increase by the amount that is mined yearly, less than the amount lost to manufacturing. In a bad year, there could actually be less of this commodity in circulation than the previous year. This is especially true of silver, where the large number of manufacturing uses deplete stocks.

Inflation is an awful thing. It increases the number of currency units in circulation, robbing, and diluting the hard-earned savings of normal people. Note, inflation is an increase in the number of currency units in circulation, not an increase in prices, despite media stories about increased prices being inflation. Even the Bank of England, perhaps accidentally, confuses the two. They often aim for an inflation 'target' of 2%, supposedly the centrally-decided ideal set of price increases for a Goldilocks, not too-warm, not too-cold, economy to function. However, when they refer to this inflation target, they mean an increase in prices. Normally, the amount of extra currency pumped into circulation yearly exceeds the 2% figure by a large margin.

After coming off the gold convertibility window in 1971, the inflation has never really stopped because there's no precious metal backing restraint at all. As the increase in currency units occurs, the most obvious way people see it is as an increase in prices and the shrinking and disappearance of coinage. In the UK, new and smaller coins are replacing the old, heavier versions, and there has been talk of stopping 1p and 2p coins completely, as has already happened to the halfpenny and farthing. There are now also cleverer accounting methods available that sound extremely cuddly and designed to help us all.

## THE OFFICIAL INFLATION RATE

When it comes to the official government inflation figures, these often understate true increases in the cost of living, due to the statistical reporting methods used. As the famous old adage goes, there are "lies, damned lies, and statistics," and nowhere could this be truer than here. One method is to reduce the real price if the assumed quality of an item included in the basket of goods has gone up in quality. For example, a 2020 computer could be classified as ten times more powerful than a 2010 computer, and even though they have the same retail price of say, £1,000; the figures are adjusted downward due to the increased processing power: whether you really needed that extra processing power, or whether it is even possible to buy a 2010 specification computer is not considered. Another method is replacement or substitution theory. As a hypothetical example, if high-quality beef rises in price, it is assumed that many households will trade down to cheaper beef, or even some other type of meat.

Whether or not these are correct ways to measure price increases in anything is open to conjecture. Still, they ultimately have the effect of making the official inflation figures lower.

## QUANTITATIVE EASING

Easing, well, that sounds good, doesn't it? Like giving room to something constrained. Literally, it means an easing on the restriction of the number of currency units in circulation.

Oh wait, so it's inflation in another form?

Well, yes. In this case, it's an extremely clever accounting trick, in which the government bonds already in circulation are bought back by the central bank, using money they just created with the touch of a button on a computer screen. Nice work if you can get it! The seller of the bonds gets an excellent price of newly-created currency in return for their bonds, and the government gets its own debt back. Do this trick enough times, and you reduce the amount of government debt in circulation, distorting the market.

This is where the mystical practice becomes even darker. While he was Chancellor of the Exchequer in the 2000s, Gordon Brown introduced laws saying that pension funds must hold a minimum percentage of their portfolio in government bonds, for 'safety' reasons. So these pension funds are committed to buying new issues of UK government bonds, almost regardless of what percentage yield the UK government offers on them.

This means that, quite possibly, your pension is committed to holding bonds with extremely low yields. Awful investments that your pension fund manager may have preferred not to hold given a chance. Meanwhile, the UK government, by buying up bonds with newly-created currency, keeps pushing bond yields down. It's not hard to see why if, say, a £1m bond from a few years ago has a yield of 5%; then if you can issue new bonds with a 1% yield, you can borrow £5m and still be making the same interest payments every month. All this borrowing also means extra currency in circulation.

Someday, this pension holding requirement could expose pension funds to a major downturn. For example, in the early 1980s, following the last gold run-up, some government bonds yields were almost 20%. If that were to be repeated, the government bonds with a 1% yield could fall to 5% of their face value. I.e., 5p in every pound. It hasn't happened yet, but history may repeat.

Just remember, when you hear 'Quantitative Easing' or 'QE,' translate it in your head to what it really means - the creation of extra currency units diluting yours. Inflation.

## INTEREST RATES

As the government controls this fiat currency, they can turn off and on the taps to create this currency by setting Interest Rates. A low-interest rate stimulates the economy by encouraging more people to borrow more money. Thus more money is issued by the lending bank, while a high-interest rate discourages more borrowing and forces repayment of existing debt.

For cash savings, low-interest rates are, of course, bad news. Still, falsely low rates as controlled by a government may win popularity with voters before an election rather than managing rates correctly. They are bad news in another, more insidious way in that they cause more inflation and thus devalue your existing savings more rapidly. As of 2020, this is exactly what is happening, with most savings accounts paying virtually zero percent in interest.

## CREATE MONEY OUT OF NOTHING

If things get really bad, you can actually just create money out of nothing by printing it. Exactly what Germany did in 1921-23, no accounting tricks needed, just turn on the printing press. This method has become even easier with digital money; just go to a computer screen, press a few buttons, and magically create the balance in your account. Governments are still wary of doing this because they know the effects it can have on borrowing and being re-electable, once an angry population realises their money is or has been destroyed. The high inflation figures at the end of the 1970s in the U.K. and

U.S.A meant regular rounds of price increases in shops. The general discontent was a major factor for the ousting of the incumbent parties and the installation of Margaret Thatcher and Ronald Reagan, respectively.

## LONG-TERM EFFECTS

The major long-term effect is that your savings are devalued. Imagine, your productivity from working is used by the bank to create new currency units for others to spend, who didn't earn it. Inflation almost inevitably leads to an increase in prices, especially when you withdraw your savings from the bank to spend them on something to benefit your own life. The longer you leave your savings there, especially with a low-interest rate, the more likely it will have happened by the time you come to spend them.

As a share investor, inflation can lead to large rises in the profits stated by businesses, and at face value, the obvious thing is to believe this is a good thing - in fact, a dose of inflation is often presented as a good thing by governments. However, when businesses need to start working on recruiting new employees or buying new stock, they find that the prices for these items have started rising, and their increased profitability was but a temporary phenomenon. In the worst cases, the raw materials to manufacture their product might actually now cost more than the price of their finished product, and they could be driven out of business.

At the worst extremes, and historically this has happened many times, a government destroys its currency by inflation. Eventually, the holders of Marks (Germany 1921-23), Livres (France 1790s), or Hungarian Pengos (1946) - the officially worst hyperinflationary currency of the twentieth century, or whatever all realise that their currency is being devalued and endeavour to get rid of it as quick as possible by buying whatever they think will hold its value instead. This makes the currency even more undesirable and worthless, which then becomes a downward spiral of which Zimbabwe is a recent prime example.

*In Germany, the banknotes were worth more as firewood by 1923*

A lesser documented effect of the inflation in Zimbabwe was that the Zimbabwean stock market rose more than the corresponding inflation, as holders of Zimbabwean dollars tried to exchange their worthless currency for something of value such as shares in reliable businesses, often with safe overseas earnings or hard assets such as property or mining rights. The conclusion to draw from this is that in times of high inflation, there are assets or businesses with pricing power that can protect you against the ravages of inflation.

The complex issue of inflation comes back to but one simple consideration for the astute investor to think about; Diversification. You probably already have some cash savings, and that is no bad thing since you will always have expenses to meet in your home country and are not so exposed to a stock market crash; plus, if a government is honest about an inflation situation and raises interest rates dramatically, then your savings have the benefit of receiving dramatic interest rates. Then there's stocks and shares - well, these might be a bumpy ride along the road of Inflationary Way, but in the end, some shares will do well out of price rises, and others will not. They certainly have a place, but to be truly diversified and protected, you should probably be holding some of your savings in the one item in world history which has always retained its purchasing power and has always been viewed as a tradable item for goods and services, and that is gold.

# GOLD AND SILVER CONFISCATION

"When plunder becomes a way of life for a group of men in a society, over the course of time, they create for themselves a legal system that authorizes it and a moral code that glorifies it."

— Frédéric Bastiat

Now you understand what inflation is, you may begin to realise that another advantage of inflation for governments is that they can collect *Capital Gains Taxes* on illusory profits made by investors. As an example, if a national currency falls in value, by say half, over some time, and the value of your investment doubles at the same time, then it might look good on paper. However, the reality is no more than the financial equivalent of standing still. In effect, it's a confiscation, but it's not the end of the story.

For, once governments got you used to the concept of using just one currency in your everyday transactions and got you used to the trust that they were looking after your gold - they began loaning it out and selling it off, often without your knowledge or consent.

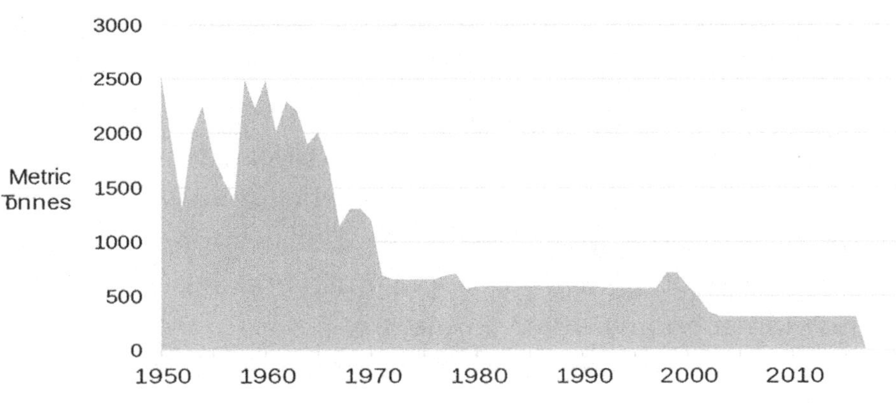


*(Chart: source: Wikipedia By Tsange - CC BY-SA 4.0)*

Looking at the chart, it's easy to see the UK gold reserves have declined massively, especially in the 1960s - leading to the famous 'Pound in your Pocket' speech by Prime Minister Harold Wilson in 1967, trying to assuage voters that their pound was still worth a pound, as the value plunged against other currencies. A pound of what, Harold? In 1999, the UK decided to sell off over half the nations' remaining gold reserves, some 400 tonnes. At the time, gold was at the end of a major 20-year bear market, and the price was at an all-time low, a price last seen in the 1970s. The Bank of England, the custodian of the countries' gold reserves, insists that it was never consulted in the decision, and some leaks, in fact, suggest that many of their staff vigorously opposed the move. They claim that Her Majesty's Treasury and them alone made the decision. At the time, the Chancellor of the Exchequer was a Mr. Gordon "Golden" Brown, who subsequently became Prime Minister.

Even worse, the huge gold sales and auctions were publicly announced well in advance, thus giving gold dealers the chance to prepare for the glut of gold that was about to be released onto the market, and force the price down still further as a result. The normal strategy is to keep intended government gold sales quiet, then simply conduct the sales on the open market, obtaining the best prices possible, then announce the results afterward.

Why might a government decide to sell off one of the main assets of its people at the lowest price possible? There were rumours and accusations that the gold was sold to prevent top Hedge Funds who had got it wrong gambling on the price of gold from going bust and destroying the worldwide economy, among others.

Regardless of the truth of the rumours, 1999-2002 has subsequently been proved to have been exactly the right time to start buying gold, not selling it; in fact, the value of the gold sold by the UK has risen by over ten *billion* dollars since that time. This period in gold price history is now referred to as 'The Brown Bottom.'

| Rank | Country | Gold Holdings (in metric tons) |
|---|---|---|
| 1 | United States of America | 8133 |
| 2 | Germany | 3363 |
| 3 | Italy | 2451 |
| 4 | France | 2436 |
| 5 | Russia | 2299 |
| 6 | China | 1948 |
| 7 | Switzerland | 1040 |
| 8 | Japan | 765 |
| 9 | India | 657 |
| 10 | Netherlands | 612 |
| 11 | Turkey | 583 |
| 12 | Taiwan | 422 |
| 13 | Portugal | 382 |
| 14 | Kazakhstan | 378 |
| 15 | Uzbekistan | 342 |
| 16 | Saudi Arabia | 323 |
| 17 | United Kingdom | 310 |
| 18 | Lebanon | 286 |
| 19 | Spain | 281 |
| 20 | Austria | 280 |

Top 20 Gold reserve nations. source: World Gold Council, August 2020

The USA meanwhile continues to report huge gold holdings of 8,133 tonnes at Fort Knox in Kentucky, the main gold storage site, built specifically in 1937 for this purpose. Is it true, though? No independent audit has been done for years. There are rumours that either all or some of the gold has been sold or loaned out. If found to be true, there could be seismic consequences for the worldwide economy.

In 2013, Germany said it wanted its gold back from storage in New York. After some negotiations, the Federal Reserve said they could have a portion back every year for x number of years. It all seemed to suggest that the gold simply wasn't there; otherwise, why not just take it away in a shorter time? It's hard to know what happened with this story, as now Germany reports it has repatriated all the gold it wishes to, but at the same time reports that 36% remains in New York. Stories like this should certainly raise alarm bells for any citizen believing that the fiat currency used in their country still has some kind of gold backing at their central bank, regardless of the officially reported reserves.

The USA did the same thing with silver, in plain sight in the twentieth century. By 1950, the USA had amassed 2 *billion* ounces of silver. In the 1960s, as industrial uses for silver increased, the government made legal moves to sell silver at a price of around $1.293 an ounce. In case you're wondering the reason for that price, it's because it equated to the value of the silver in a silver dollar. Had it gone higher, there'd be another case of Gresham's Law. By 1967, the USA had sold 80% of its silver, and in 1970 it officially stopped selling. By June 1973, it was $3 an ounce - yes, precious metals held by your government, supposedly on your behalf, were selling for three times the price they offloaded it at, just 10 years later. Silver had a spell of decline in the mid-1970s, but finished the decade on a high, having reached almost $50:-

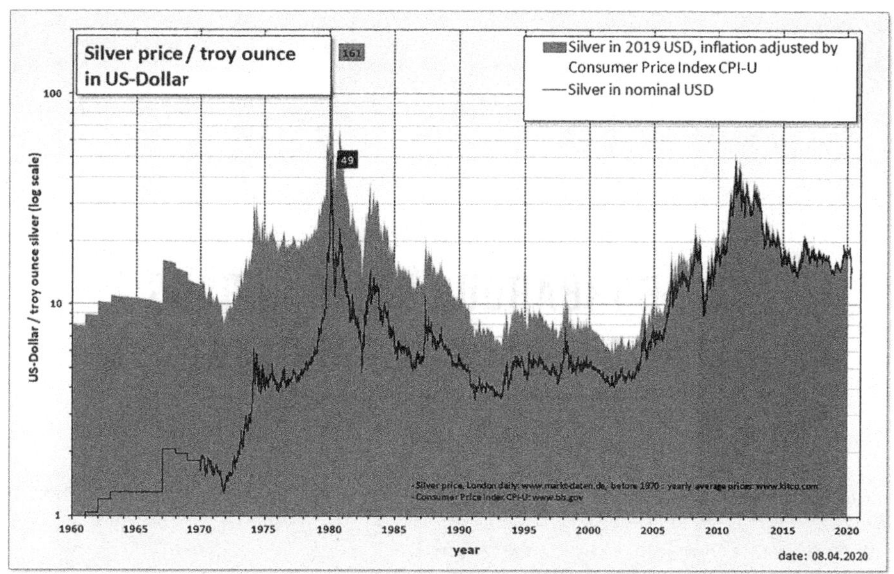


*(Chart: Silver performance, 1960-2000, with 1980 spike.*
*Source: Wikipedia, Realterm/CC BY-SA)*

# THE BARBAROUS RELIC VERSUS THE BARBAROUS PRIVILEGE

"In truth, the gold standard is already a barbarous relic."

— John Maynard Keynes, 1924

Prescient words indeed, by John Maynard Keynes in 1924. Inflation had already happened with the increases in the currency in circulation during World War 1. The market was merely trying to adjust to the new reality by now, and in 1926, the gold window at the bank of England officially closed. For the last time. The British Pound as a unit of solid value was finished.

There's some of a crossover here between the three strands of gold, silver, and freedom during the 1900s-1930s period.

Number one, the theft of the real wealth behind your savings, the gold, is almost complete. A sleight-of-hand, carried out by master magicians behind a curtain while you were distracted and through a variety of stooges, fooled into looking the other way while it happened. That extreme crises like wars and depressions are often the times the tricks are done, or the trick at least begins is not a total surprise. After all, it's at this time people are most amenable to autosuggestion, through their fear and rush of adrenalin telling them to flee or fight.

Number two, the silver. The florins, shillings, and sixpences are still in circulation but will begin their dilution in the UK at least, in the 1940s and the USA, in the 1960s. In a few hundred years, we'll have gone from owning the wealth to having tokens representing the wealth, then behind the scenes having the wealth removed. In the 1990s, the move to digital currency means we will even begin to lose the metal value of the tokens, and the money will be backed by nothing but trust. Mutual trust that someone will continue to accept your Pounds, Dollars, or Euros in exchange for goods and services. A trust so shallow that it has to be enforced by law.

Number three, Freedom itself. A couple of major moves were introduced around this time that now began to erode this aspect of our lives. Passports and a command economy.

Now, think about how easy travel was before 1914. Trains crossed international borders; people took ships to faraway places where they often intended to begin new lives and never return. In Europe, comparatively few people had passports, even if they travelled to other countries. Then World War 1 came, and it all changed. Britain introduced the 'Nationality and status of Aliens Act' in 1914. Many countries interned citizens of opposing nations who happened to live within their borders for the duration of the war. When the war ended, the passports never went away. A League of Nations conference in 1920 made them a fact of life. The USA, formerly very welcoming to immigrants, introduced laws like the 1924 immigration act to restrict newcomers. There are stories that many people were not happy about the photographs and information on passports they were expected to provide.

Many US citizens felt the same about the introduction of Social Security numbers. Data protection and privacy were issues, even back then. The issues around data are covered further in **Data is The New Oil.**

World War 1 was also a great exercise in introducing a command economy on nation-states. Nations got used to having large amounts of money to spend and distribute. People got used to being told what they could and couldn't buy, or even what job they had to do. As well as being told that it was all happening for their own good. Even freer countries took this route, as the 1930s gold confiscation in the USA and subsequent large government spending on Roosevelt's New Deal prove. The economic theories of John Maynard Keynes were very helpful in selling this to the public.

## KEYNESIANISM

In case you don't know who John Maynard Keynes was, a brief introduction is necessary. He was an economist who believed in something called *aggregate demand*. Whereas up to World War 1, the economy had been left to some extent to manage itself; he believed that recessions could be avoided. Full employment could be maintained permanently by the government, making up the shortfall if there was a recession. His theories really found their place in the 1930s, when all governments began trying them out to get the economy going after the Wall Street crash of 1929. Whether they were successful or not is open to debate, as the small matter of World War 2 came along and put world economies on an entirely different footing to before.

This is where the running of household finances and government finances begin to diverge. You may remember that back in the gold standard days, both households and nations saw value in saving more and spending less. Now the government wants to spend the way to prosperity. Now, think about this approach for a second and ask yourself how it would work if you run your household like this - as an *aggregate demand* household. To do this, what you need to do is try to spend an identical amount of money every week, or month, regardless of what your real expenses are. Furthermore, if your household income declines, then no matter, just take out a loan and keep your aggregate demand running at the same level you did before. On those days where you're failing to spend up to the exact limit, then no worries, just pop up the shop, buy some excess food and throw it in the bin, just to keep aggregate demand constant. Honestly, does this seem like a sound economic principle to you?

Probably not. Yet, it's exactly how your government operates. For Keynes is still a very popular figure in the world of government today. All governments nowadays are Keynesian and convinced that with enough government spending, any recession or lull in the economy can be averted. It's a bit like paying everyone to endlessly sweep roads in a way, whether they are dirty or not. . Still, they've often gone way beyond it, with spending just to stimulate the economy for many different reasons, for example, a feel-good boost just before an important election. The other side of the Keynesian theory was that when there's inflation, the government should turn the taps off and reduce demand. It seems that governments nowadays forgot that second part. Keynes probably turns in his grave at the misuse of his name in these situations - he wasn't totally a fan of banking tricks, as can be seen by his quote in **Fiat Currency.**

Of course, as you know from **Inflation**, governments have more sophisticated access to funds than you do, but it doesn't help. Whatever methods they use, they are still pumping extra currency units into circulation and devaluing those currency units already in existence. It erodes one simple yet important basis of human society - savings. For those currency units being devalued by the new entrants are most likely to be yours and others like you, who've saved them away from your past productivity to use on some future event - a general backup, a holiday, a new car, or the college education fund. You expect that you will be able to dip into those savings at some point in the future when the need arises and that those savings will have the same or very similar value as they did before. You may have realised that the creation by the government of extra currency units, competing for goods and services with yours, has lessened the chances of that happening.

Some economists nowadays are more open to questioning the efficacy of Keynesian methods. However, even today, few at the governmental level seem to have noticed or care and continue the same approach. They especially went for it wholesale during the 2008-09 financial crisis. Nor has it registered that Japan has been doing these policies for 30 years now, since their stock market crashed in 1989 and it hasn't worked. The country has many examples of government projects, like bridges to small islands, that would never be economically viable, but were built simply to provide employment and get the economy moving again.

Keynes lives on today in the UK town of 'Milton Keynes,' a 1960s new town named in his honour. However, if, as he said, gold is the 'Barbarous relic,' then fiat currency is the 'barbarous privilege.' The barbarous privilege to dictate that the citizens of a country transact in a single elastic currency by decree, a currency that the dictator* can turn on or off the taps for, impoverishing the citizens and possibly even enriching themselves, if they know the next move planned.

Any sensible saver will prefer the barbarous relic over the barbarous privilege.[1]

---

1    In the sense of someone who dictates, or tells you to do something.

# PART 2

# SOCIAL INSECURITY

"Those who would give up essential Liberty to purchase a little temporary Safety deserve neither Liberty nor Safety."

— Benjamin Franklin

It's interesting the USA also pursued Keynesian policies in the same period, with Roosevelt's 'New Deal,' employing workers on huge government projects like the Hoover Dam. What rarely is mentioned, however, is how those projects were funded. They had confiscated the gold of the population back in 1933, then issued extra currency against the gold that now sat in their hands, currency they could decide what to do with. In other words, *Inflation*. In this respect, with ownership of the gold in a central vault and now having lots of paper dollars to spend on pet projects, it can be viewed as a huge theft from the American people and a huge reordering of societal values. The Keynesian economics of the 1930s and the acceptance by the population of an outside force helping 'improve' their lives led to a whole new phase of economics, another mindset switch for the population, where, during 1939-45, the central government assumed the power to decide what you could eat, spend money on and even gave you a gun and ordered you to kill other humans you'd never met before, on the threat of prison. The control didn't even end in 1945 - the last rationing in the U.K. continued until 1951.

## AN INSPECTOR CALLS

After World War 2, it was no surprise the welfare state emerged and, with it, a whole load of new money distribution schemes. Setting the scene, there had just been a major war, and the people of the UK were weary. After all, what had they got out of it? There had to be something back in return for their sacrifices, didn't there? That was what led to the ousting of Prime Minister Winston Churchill and the installation of a new Labour PM, Clement Atlee, in 1945.

"An Inspector Calls" is a 1945 play by J.B. Priestley, but based in Edwardian England, around 1910. There's a poignant scene in which a poor commoner goes to the local poor council to ask for needed funds as she has lost her job and is pregnant. The unpleasant Mrs Birling, the wife of a well-to-do local industrialist, sits on the council and decides that this woman is undeserving of help, totally on her own personal whims. The woman dies later. Or does she? If you've not seen this play or film dramatisation, it is highly recommended. Priestley presented this scene to support the introduction of a more socialist regime in the UK. Espousing free universal healthcare, regardless of circumstances.

The National Health Service, in particular, sounded wonderful. Free universal healthcare in the UK was introduced in 1946. The idea of free healthcare for everyone indeed did work well, right up to the 1970s, to some extent, when it even rescued the author of this book. Thank you. However, since the 1980s, it has been twisted and contorted into something largely unrelated to health and care, but increasingly means large profits for corporations from construction, sub-contracted services, and medical products like pharmaceuticals. In **The Crown** and **50 Percent a Slave**, you will find more on this. It was never free, of course. Taxpayers paid for it through something new called "National Insurance." In a way, maybe that was fine to say after what you've been through, give us extra, and we will use that specifically to give you and your family healthcare, money when you are unemployed, and the promise of a pension back when you retire. As long as they delivered on those promises, perhaps.

## MARY POPPINS

For a while, they did. Everyone was happy. Underneath, though, something had changed. It only becomes apparent many years later what. The government had now put itself in the position of a Nanny, looking after dependent children. That's the thing with a nanny; it's still an appointed authority. Although nanny was lenient in the early years, largely looking after everyone, always smiling like Mary Poppins and saying yes to most with their requests for help, she began to change. She started inventing new rules, cutting the benefits paid out, reducing the pensions paid, and she even began talking about her hospitals not treating you for certain ailments. The self-same hospitals that, ironically enough, you had paid to build and be staffed, should you need them.

The irony of the Priestley play and the judgemental way in which welfare is issued or not issued to the needy recipient should not be lost on modern Britain, as the government now acts as a much larger version of Mrs Birling. Deciding, almost arbitrarily with an iron fist, on whether someone gets help or not. Again, media commentary exists in the form of the 2016 Ken Loach film "I, Daniel Blake," where someone who loses their work begins a downward life spiral, with his benefits gradually cut for failing to abide by Nanny's rules. Even when those failures were for valid reasons. A cautionary tale for anyone thinking Nanny cares about them.

The other sad thing is those people who had money extracted from them in return for services that they will never receive, for it is rather clear that state pensions will either not exist, be means-tested, or be of extremely nominal value in the not-too-distant future. That translates into most of us. As usual, it was a financial sleight-of-hand, in which the government promised to invest the contributions. 'Contributions' sounds so much softer than extractions, since the contributors had little choice, into a fund. The sad thing is that the fund was never actually created, and the extractions just went into the central pot to be spent on the latest schemes of the day.

The worst part of it all? The appointment of a Nanny inevitably means an erosion of the parent's role in looking after children. Silently, stealthily, that is exactly what has happened. Now Nanny began encroaching on the rest of your wealth, setting new rules, and generally getting her finger in every pie. For example, your children, in many ways, represent one of your ultimate forms of family silver, yet now the government seems to have turned its attention onto those too. In Germany, the Measles vaccine for children is now mandatory, and in Australia, Nanny has set rules that parents who decide not to get their children vaccinated will get deductions in their welfare. In terms of wealth confiscation, nothing matters more than our children. Yet, the figures for children taken into care are rising massively every year, with a whole new industry of care homes and foster families undermining the traditional family unit. Divorce statistics have also risen dramatically. More symptoms of hiring a nanny, perhaps?

**Marriage & Divorce Rates in the United States**
(per 1,000 population)



*(Chart: divorce rates USA)*

Taken this way, nanny not only seems to have caused a lot of divorces with her ample welfare charms but in the 1980s, she began to become so omnipresent, many people don't even bother getting married in the first place anymore.

## LIVING UNDER RULES

Whether we knew we agreed to it or not, we now live in a system where the state has set rules and continues to invent new ones. Rules as to whether we can receive any money when we are employed, what healthcare we receive when ill, and what money we receive when old. If any. By taking money from us to pay for it, we were also left too impoverished in many cases to make our own provisions on each of these items because of those extra payments. It got the population used to money on tap, as long as you followed someone else's rules. For example, many newly-redundant coal miners and steelworkers in the UK in the 1980s went on a mission to spend as much of their redundancy money as possible, as quickly as possible, to be below the savings limit for obtaining unemployment benefits. The exact opposite of what individual households would probably have done by choice. Yes, the population definitely has got used to following rules set by someone else. Rules that come with many penalties and threats if not followed and even still, some rewards if followed. An important factor for later chapters.

Whether it was intended to or not, what has happened is that we all traded our liberty in return for a small piece of security most of us never truly use, nor would many of us be able to use it if we needed to anymore. However, Nanny is still there, her shadow growing over us every day, and she's not going away any time soon. In fact, the shadow just got worse in 2020, when Nanny started deciding major aspects of our lives, including when and why we are even allowed to leave the house or meet with friends and relatives.

# THE CROWN

"We Should Be Happier To Have A Job Than To Have Savings"

— Christine Lagarde, 2019.

Thank you, Christine. Your quote is the main reason why "How to Invest in Gold and Silver" got revisited 13 years after the original publication. Gold had underperformed for many years after attaining an all-time high in 2012, and gold mining companies had declined massively. Meanwhile, stock markets were apparently flying along and hitting new highs daily. Commodity prices were now lower than ever, in many cases and there was doubt in the premise of that book still being valid. Perhaps the 2008-09 crisis and fallout really was over?

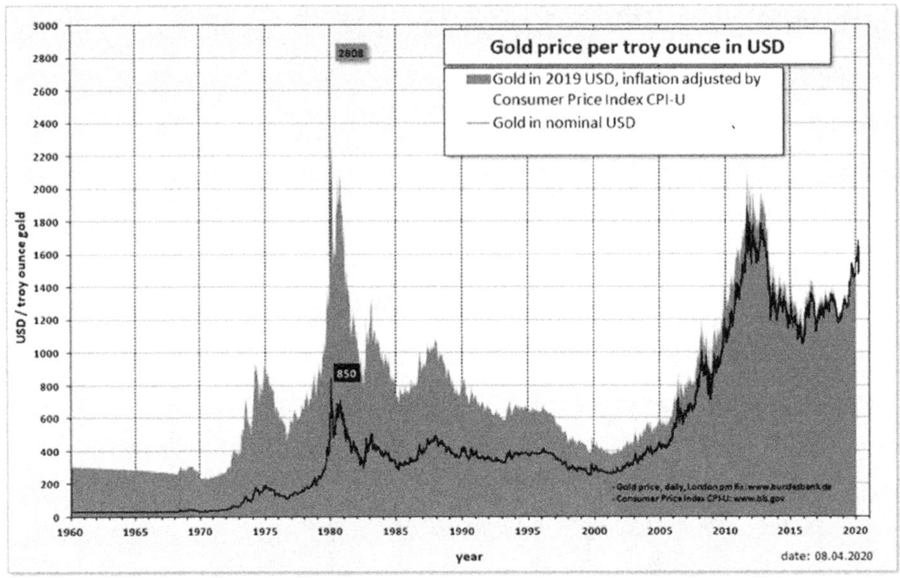


*(Chart of Gold price 1960-2000, source: Wikipedia, Realterm CC)*

When Christine said that, though, it was time to wonder. For those who don't know Christine Lagarde, she makes big decisions on finance at the ECB (European Central Bank). The ECB is the banking facet of the European Union, and she was appointed to lead it in 2019. It doesn't seem to matter that she was convicted of a financial crime 4 years earlier, nor did she seem to suffer any penalty for the conviction. Christine attends many events where big-ticket items are discussed, but no agenda or minutes of meetings are made public - think Bilderbergs and the World Economic Forum, for example. Christine even has Hollywood links - she was interviewed in 2010 as part of the documentary "Inside Job," helping explain how those awful banks played roulette with our mortgages, savings, and investments, and it was all their fault. Lone financial gunmen, acting alone.

In summary, Ms Lagarde is a big cheese - or fromage grande to use her own language. When she says something, you can believe it may not just be her own words and possibly comes from somewhere deeper.

So ask yourself now, what does this quote mean to you? Images of savings being destroyed and life being a treadmill of working to earn enough to survive? Working on this premise, but not knowing what was coming or how that would be achieved, it was hard to know what to do except ensuring you have some diversification, then watch and wait.

In early 2020 it began to be clearer.

## BACKGROUND

A new virus hit the world. A virus so, so awful that nanny said we had to stay indoors. We couldn't go near another person, go to work, school, visit a shop or travel anywhere. Life turned upside down. For millions, their livelihoods just stopped instantly. Unemployment rates flew up, and western governments especially introduced emergency payments to those now finding themselves out of work. Emergency payments that continue to the present day. In countries without the European levels of welfare, such as India, trains just stopped in their tracks. Leaving many workers who travel across the country to simply try and walk hundreds of miles home, with no financial means of support. For the luckier ones, offices worldwide closed, but they were allowed to continue working, albeit from home. It was a virus that also hammered stock markets across the world down by 40% or more.

If you feel you've heard the story before, then it may be because you watched the 2011 film 'Contagion,' in which a disease hit the world, killing thousands, stopping everything, and striking fear and distrust into everyone worldwide. This film had all the ingredients you might expect to find. The heroes, desperately trying to save lives and find a vaccine, like Kate Winslet. The villains, like the odd-toothed conspiracy theorist Alan Krumwiede, played by Jude Law, who gets his just desserts when he dies trying to prove the virus isn't real. The film is quite clear on who is good and who is bad, in typical Hollywood style, and ends by showing how the virus began in a pig farm in China, started by bats. If that bit sounds really familiar, it's because you may have heard it used in 2020 as a possible explanation of how Corona (*Spanish, English Translation*: Crown) began.

The gist of the film is certainly that only a vaccine is the solution, and in one week of August 2020, during travels across countries, the following line, from acquaintances and TV was heard, *Ad Infinitum*:-

"Life won't get back to normal until we get a vaccine."

So there we go, there's a big illness, and the people are being primed to take what they are told is the remedy.

## BUSINESS AND FINANCE

Now, it's way outside the remit of this book to question the medical aspects of the virus, but we can certainly look at the economic aspects concerning money. Certainly, stock markets fell dramatically and in a very short time.

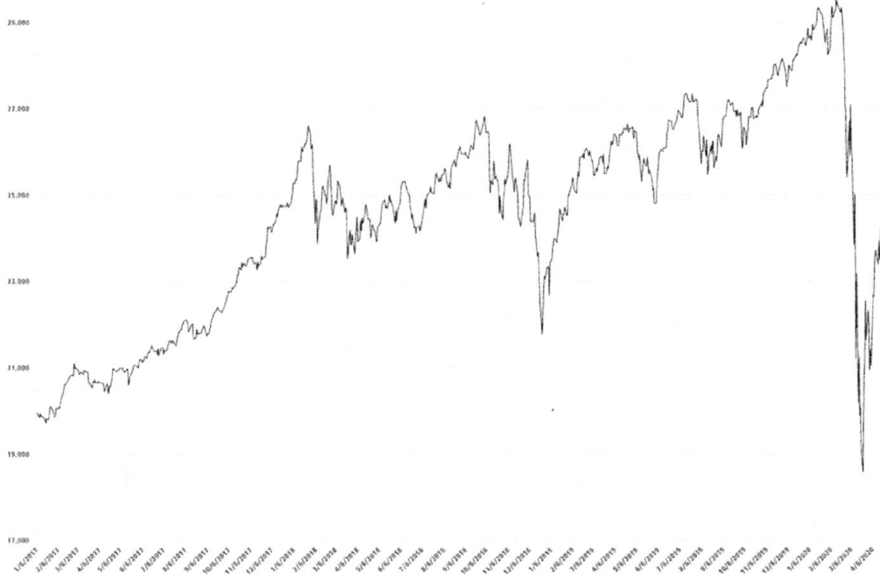

*(Chart: NYSE 2017-2020, showing 2020 crash,
source: Wikipedia, Locke Cole CC 3.0)*

Conversely, gold and silver have risen dramatically since the pandemic was announced.

*(Chart: Gold performance 2010-2020)*

As one response to the crisis, the USA eliminated the reserve lending requirements of **fractional reserve banking** completely. In other words, if banks wish to grant a loan, they can just go to a computer terminal, press a button, and hey presto! Money created out of thin air with interest added. Even with fractional reserve banking, there was some remote semblance of the money needing to be attached to something, in terms of deposits. As you now realise, this is nothing more than theft via a dilution of the value of your savings, due to the increased number of currency units now in circulation. This will have been noted by some investors, for sure, and explain some of the rises in precious metals.

In case you wonder about the true value of gold and silver as money, perhaps it's worth cutting fiat currency out of the equation completely and looking at gold versus the DJIA. Measured in gold, the crash looks a bit different, since gold, the true money has also risen versus fiat currency. Unlike the fiat money recovery of the stock market since the middle of 2020, the market has remained down versus gold.

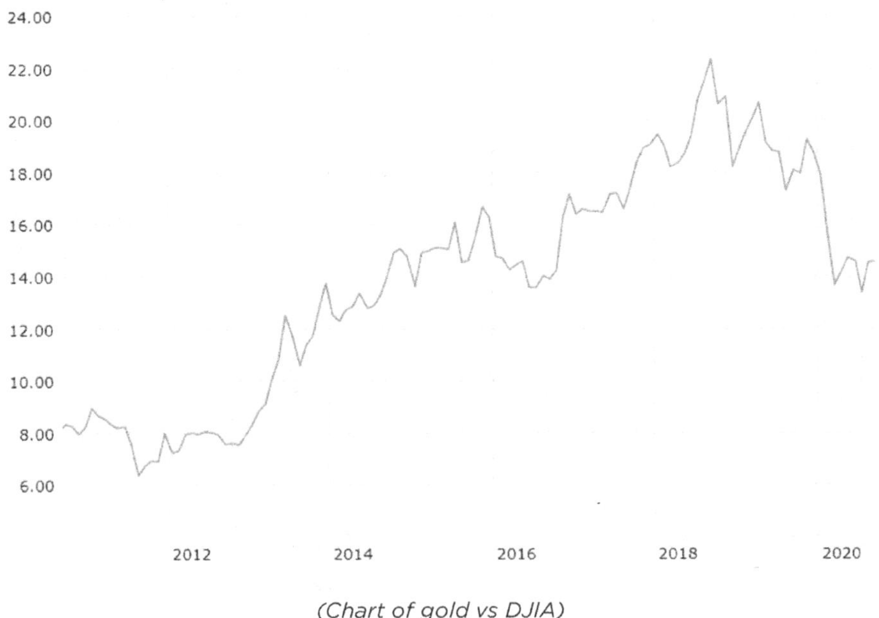

*(Chart of gold vs DJIA)*

It wasn't all bad news for businesses and the stock markets, though. Some business sectors were clear winners:-

- Technology - Work from home, shop from home, socialise from home. The crisis is a bonanza for technology companies. Their success, plus possible future trends, are covered in **Data is New Oil.**

- Pharmaceuticals - "It won't get back to normal until we get a vaccine." They are now developing and selling a lot more products. Sometimes with the research risk removed by even having it funded by governments.

- Supermarkets - With no dining out and no socialising, eating at home has become the "new normal." Footage of queues and fights for toilet rolls was a staple media news item in the early days.

- Banks - Being able to distribute government money, defer customer loan repayments, and having an ultimate charge on properties if loan repayments are not made, especially in a period of **Deflation,** could be a major factor later in the crisis.

The strength and power of the corporations will be covered in greater detail in **The Road from Democracy to Corporatocracy.**

The World Economic Forum (WEF) was founded by the German Klaus Schwab in 1971 and is based in Geneva, Switzerland. You may know it most as the hosts of the yearly "Davos" conference, oft-reported on the media, where political and financial heavyweights meet to discuss pressing matters of the day. The truly global reach of this organisation is shown by a board of trustees that includes Al Gore, Mark Carney, and Jack Ma. It now openly refers to this period of uncertainty, illness, and death as 'The Great Reset' via their website. Articles it posts give some clues that business and life may not return to how it was before. The oft-quoted phrase of the era, "The New Normal," which you may have heard many places, suggests big changes too. What this may mean is covered in future chapters and **Into The Future**.

## GENERAL WELFARE

In **The Barbarous Relic versus the Barbarous privilege** and **Social Insecurity**, we looked at how it gradually became socially acceptable for a government to run a command economy and to distribute currency to citizens based on certain criteria. This crisis has invented a whole new multitude of ways to distribute money to favoured interests and individuals. In addition to being unemployed, you can now get your full salary for doing nothing, while someone else you worked with has to continue to do their job, on the same salary, with all of the commitments their job requires. In many cases, it goes way beyond those in employment - the self-employed can also make claims to get their earnings covered. Staying at home, being paid full salary, having all the time in the world to do the house up, improve the garden, or even find another job to boost your earnings even more - a concept in the UK that has become affectionately known as "double-dipping." It all sounds idyllic, doesn't it, but there must be a catch, and, of course, there is.

If the various schemes introduced to pay employed people to do nothing sound like a major extension to the welfare system, then that's probably because they are. Some people were bound to question the point in being productive, when for the same amount of money you could do nothing. Not everyone will feel that way, and some will be upset and stressed about the loss of work, but in terms of bending minds, taking power from people, and getting them used to rules, it is very reminiscent of the 1980s deindustrialisation of Northern England. A period when hopelessness and despair took over from community, self-sufficiency, and a strong work ethic. The schemes may also be the start of something that has been thrown around for several years now and never gained traction - *Universal Basic Income*. The concept of Universal Basic Income (UBI) is quite simple - every citizen is issued with a basic amount of government fiat currency per year, enough to live on. It never caught on because too many people could see through it - whatever the UBI level is, it would become the new zero, and self-sufficiency and freedom would surely be eroded. To say nothing of the existing gold base supporting more and more newly issued currency units every year.

Where the extra fiat currency has come from to fund all, this is hard to see any real statistics on. We know that at some point, public borrowing must rise, and indeed, that is being presented through the news to make it palatable to the public, but increasing borrowing takes time. Wherever it came from, the consequence of these policies must be **Inflation**. Quite simply put, there must be a lot more currency units in circulation than there were a year ago, and even if the majority of those units are in bank accounts right now, doing nothing, at some point, they will begin to enter the market and circulate. At that point, prices must begin to rise. Whether this happens tomorrow or in a few years seems to be the only question.

The other inflationary aspect of this crisis is the creation of new laws, rules, and regulations. Many of them, with the intention of separating people from each other, ostensibly to prevent the virus from spreading. All countries seem to have introduced them, and many seem to have introduced very similar ones. This will be covered more in **50 Percent a Slave**.

## CURRENCY DELIVERY AND PAYMENT

The whole crisis has shown how digital the world has become concerning money. The furlough scheme is a major example in itself. UK Businesses were expected to log their furlough claims using the internet. The IT infrastructure and software to support this was in place in record time - major IT projects can often take months or years to design, develop, thoroughly test, and release. It's then an example of how the currency can now be distributed quickly to millions, through the central government, to businesses, then distributed electronically to customer accounts in banking computers. Not a single physical coin or note ever having existed.

Many other nations introduced a furlough scheme, but the USA did not. In this case, they mailed out Corona stimulus cheques of $1,200 to everyone. Lamenting, while doing so, that it was a shame that it was taking longer because they needed to get signatures on every cheque. Then, that it would have been so much easier had they had more direct banking details, such as a nominated bank account, to send the money out to the recipients electronically. Given what is explained soon, these hints become even more relevant.

As to spending, well, more and more of it became electronic as internet shopping took off even further. Still, some preferred physical currency to a certain extent. However, one of the early casualties of Corona has been cash - the number of shops now insisting on electronic payments only and media stories saying that cash can help spread the disease is a clear signal that the system no longer wants people using old-fashioned coins and notes. Also, remember Gresham's law about bad money forcing out good? There is probably a case that people are genuinely retaining more banknotes and coins at home, just if they are needed for some kind of emergency.

So this where we are at - you most likely receive your fiat credits electronically into a bank account, whatever the source. Then, most likely, spend it electronically using plastic cards, online transactions, and direct debits. With an occasional cash transaction and perhaps you even have a mobile payment app on your smartphone. The methods may have changed, but Life on the surface remains much as it has always been. As Charles Dickens noted nearly two hundred years ago:-

"Annual income twenty pounds, annual expenditure nineteen and six, result happiness. Annual income twenty pounds, annual expenditure twenty pounds nought and six, result in misery."

*Charles Dickens, David Copperfield*

The only difference is that instead of looking at a paper ledger or bank statement showing income and expenses, you are more likely to be viewing it now via an electronic screen. However, the future may be about to change dramatically, with direct delivery of currency to the human body itself, via wifi and the new, much-heralded 5G mobile network. Time to introduce Patent WO2020060606A1, filed in June 2019 by Microsoft and published on 26 March 2020, while Corona events began to dominate the news. What follows is the official abstract from the google patents page.

"Human body activity associated with a task provided to a user may be used in a mining process of a cryptocurrency system. A server may provide a task to a device of a user which is communicatively coupled to the server. A sensor communicatively coupled to or comprised in the device of the user may sense body activity of the user. Body activity data may be generated based on the sensed body activity of the user. The cryptocurrency system communicatively coupled to the device of the user may verify if the body activity data satisfies one or more conditions set by the cryptocurrency system and award cryptocurrency to the user whose body activity data is verified."

Now, as we're moving into the future here, the conversation turns hypothetical - If the entities behind this Patent wished to wire up the human body to be able to function in this manner, how could they do it? How would they get people to agree to accept it?

It's up to you to think about that but consider this. The person behind Microsoft, William Gates III, also runs a Bill and Melinda Gates Foundation (Melinda being his wife), that pays out billions to projects of their choosing. Wikipedia may have more up to date figures by the time you read this, but a flavour is as follows:-

The following table lists the top receiving organizations to which the Bill & Melinda Gates Foundation has committed funding, between 2009 and 2015. The table only includes grants recorded in the Gates Foundation's IATI publications.

| Organization | Amount ($ millions) |
| --- | ---: |
| GAVI Alliance | 3,152.8 |
| World Health Organization | 1,535.1 |
| The Global Fund to Fight AIDS, Tuberculosis and Malaria | 777.6 |
| PATH | 635.2 |
| United States Fund for UNICEF | 461.1 |
| The Rotary Foundation of Rotary International | 400.1 |
| International Bank for Reconstruction and Development | 340.0 |
| Global Alliance for TB Drug Development | 338.4 |
| Medicines for Malaria Venture | 334.1 |
| PATH Vaccine Solutions | 333.4 |
| UNICEF Headquarters | 277.6 |
| Johns Hopkins University | 265.4 |
| Aeras | 227.6 |
| Clinton Health Access Initiative Inc | 199.5 |
| International Development Association | 174.7 |
| CARE | 166.2 |
| World Health Organization Nigeria Country Office | 166.1 |
| Agence française de développement | 165.0 |
| Centro Internacional de Mejoramiento de Maíz y Trigo | 153.1 |
| Cornell University | 146.7 |
| Alliance for a Green Revolution in Africa | 146.4 |
| United Nations Foundation | 143.0 |
| University of Washington Foundation | 138.2 |
| Foundation for the National Institutes of Health | 136.2 |
| Emory University | 123.2 |
| University of California San Francisco | 123.1 |
| Population Services International | 122.5 |
| University of Oxford | 117.8 |
| International Food Policy Research Institute | 110.7 |
| International Institute of Tropical Agriculture | 104.8 |

*Source: Wikipedia, August 2020*

You are invited to research for yourselves the organisations on this list. As a flavour, the single biggest contribution goes to GAVI - The Global Alliance for Vaccine and Immunization. The second-biggest contribution goes to the WHO - The World Health Organisation. The WHO is often presented as a league of nations-type organisation, but the second-biggest contributor behind the USA to the WHO is not a nation-state. It is the Bill and Melinda Gates Foundation.

That Nations are following World Health Organisation guidelines on Corona, including the push for vaccines, when it's second-biggest contributor is linked to what would be a very, very profitable patent if the appropriate technology can be placed into the human body should be asked about by the government and media, on behalf of everyone. Wherever you live, you may have recently heard an interview with Bill Gates by your national media during these times. One day, a well-known BBC presenter conducted such an interview. Gates was presented as a Pandemic expert, despite having no formal qualifications of that kind. Then, GAVI was mentioned by the presenter, with no mention of how it is linked. Nor was there any mention of this cryptocurrency patent at all. In the USA, an interview between Ellen and Bill Gates on a similar vein was taken down from Facebook after receiving thousands of critical comments, many of them asking questions like those just mentioned. The internet was meant to lead to the sharing of more information and greater knowledge amongst the population, but it seems that investigative journalism is weakening. This is indeed not a criticism of Gates, nor Microsoft. Most of us use their products every single day. By choice. Gates himself would probably love to face genuine public inquisition to help prove that there is no conflict of interest.

It's also impossible to ignore the biblical aspect of this patent number. WO2020 - New World Order 2020 and

060606 - 666. Either it's a coincidence, someone is having a major joke, or a biblical prophecy is playing out in front of our eyes.

> "And that no man might buy or sell, save he that had the mark, or the name of the beast, or the number of his name."

> — Revelation 13:17

Media stories have been appearing in the last few years, too, on related subjects. Showing, for example, how some Swedes are taking microchips in the skin that can be used to make payments in shops. This is presented as being easier than having a plastic card in a wallet. Sweden is very advanced down the cashless society route, with some shops not taking cash payments at all. Along with stories of people being chipped by employers to get access to their place of employment, these may well be clues about the future technologies that we will have to make decisions about whether we want them in our bodies or not. Assuming we still have that right to decide for ourselves. It could indeed be *in our DNA*, and soon.

It sounds extreme at first, but when you step back and think, then you may realise you, or others you know, have been close to this already. Here are some steps to think about:-

1) Wearable technology. Beginning with the simple pedometers that counted your steps, then moving to smartwatches and smart scales, all integrated to give you an overview of your health

2) Improved mobile phone data gathering on journey's undertaken and step counting. When carried in the pocket, mobiles are even detecting floors travelled up and down and giving more statistics

3) The Nintendo Wii, with the handheld controller, your arm movements were detectable for playing games like bowls. Then there were voice sensors to validate your singing against the computer and even a Wii-fit board that could sense your movements

4) The Pokemon craze of 2017, where children and some adults got hooked on a new app on their mobiles that involved visiting real locations to collect virtual rewards

It seems human beings love a good game, especially ones that can be counted and perhaps involve an element of measurement versus other human beings to define success or failure. The Pokemon game was actually quite close to what is being proposed, in some ways. It only seems to have two major differences - you could collect the points or rewards, but they weren't usable as a cybercurrency, and it was possible to cheat. For example, people soon realised they could carry a few mobiles to collect the elusive ones on behalf of their friends. The only extra steps would be to make the collected rewards have value and to remove the ability to cheat the system. One way might be to have a tracker in the human body itself, bluetoothing to the phone to prove it's you. Another, perhaps, nanotechnology in the body to check actual activities are undertaken. Now, think back to how successful the Pokemon game was in gaining traction with the general population, especially children. Is it really so far-fetched?

Hollywood similarities are found with the 2011 film "In Time," starring Justin Timberlake. In this film, people have a built-in microchip clock-type device on their arm to top up and spend credits with. The clock is constantly ticking down in real-time, too, just by living, and people are forced to commit crimes to steal time from other humans to survive. Overall, a rather dystopian future is presented, where people are always conscious of their need to earn time just to survive another day. It's noticeable in this film, too, that extra credits are given out to favoured interests by the overlords running the system and deducted from others. A likely increased future feature of currency issuance, as technological advances continue.

In conclusion, if you think having technology embedded in your body to support a new currency system is a great idea, then don't worry because through inertia on your part, it may well be what you will get. Bear in mind, though, that under the new cybercurrency regime, inertia probably won't earn you any credits. Writing reviews praising the cybercurrency issuer may well earn you credits, as may other activities considered 'correct.' Writing public comments questioning certain things may just as easily get you deductions. Basically, someone else may decide what credits you get and what credits get deducted directly from your body. They might also have an off switch in there if your life is deemed unworthy by the death panel.

If this doesn't sound like utopia to you, then it's certainly worth considering what kind of future relationship we want with the money and what relationships we don't want. That is covered later, but for now, things may get darker...

# THE ROAD FROM DEMOCRACY TO CORPORATOCRACY

"If Corporations Are People, They Are Psychopaths"

— The movie The Corporation, 2003.

The concept of corporations goes back to Roman times and possibly still further. The basic idea is that a group of people got together to form a venture. Normally with profit-bearing motives. The word 'corporation' even comes from the Latin, 'corpus,' meaning 'group of people.' Part of the idea of corporations being that the venture could live on beyond the lifespans of normal people. Corporations really caught on as imperial trade ventures spread further and further afield, growing with the globalisation and taking us to the point today where these huge entities dominate national stock markets and their corporate footprint is everywhere. Most visibly seen in the products we buy and the logos we see all the time.

In terms of the relationship between governments, corporations, and the people, the view seems to be that the government is paternalistically representing the people and that corporations are off to the side regulated and taxed by the government, and people have the choice of whether or not to transact with them. In a way, they are almost considered to be a subset of the people, in the respect that many also own shares in the corporations, either directly or through their pooled investment schemes, like pensions. Also, people believe that the government is voted in by and represents the people, and the people only.

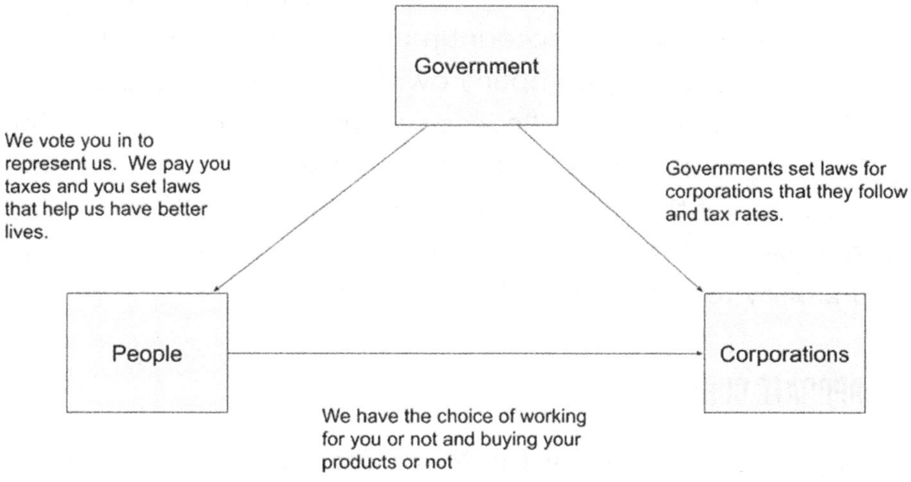


*(Chart: How people think it works)*

This old-fashioned view is questionable. Big business has a lot more say in how things are run than you might think. The field of business itself has also become a very slanted playing field - the larger a corporation is, the more capable it is of using offshore and international jurisdictions to minimise its tax liability in any given country. This gives larger corporations a huge advantage over smaller, single-country, or even physical, single-town competitors, who must pay local taxes and therefore have a lot less to reinvest into the business in future years. The doubly sad aspect of this being that the reinvestment would probably be made locally, helping lift the community overall. Citizens are often frustrated by the apparent ability of the big corporations to dance rings about government tax collection using these methods that are unavailable to smaller businesses and individuals. For example, In the UK in 2010, HMRC waived a potential tax bill of £7bn from Vodafone. David Hartnett, the head of HMRC at the time, even later admitted that he might have made mistakes in some of his actions while settling potential high-yield tax disputes with multinational companies. Also, Vodafone sold its stake in Verizon Wireless in 2013, to Verizon Communications in the USA. When it came to accounting for taxes, it claimed that a Netherlands Holding company owned the shares sold outside of UK tax jurisdiction and consequently paid no tax. This is all entirely legal, of course, and not a criticism of any corporation doing this, but the net effect of these kinds of deals on smaller businesses and citizens themselves is a bigger tax burden and an inability to compete fairly.

## CORPORATE CURRENCY

Now, let's consider what the Microsoft cybercurrency patent possibly represents - a form of currency issued by a corporation. While corporate currencies aren't really considered much in today's society, they already exist in several forms. For example, every time you take a flight, you earn air miles. The air miles are deemed to have a certain fiat currency value in dollars or euros, but their real value is in exchangeability with the airline for buying their flights and is a much higher value that cannot be covered by the nominal fiat currency value. With corporate currencies, you are also trusting in the continued existence of the corporation and, furthermore, the continued exchangeability of the corporate currency for goods and services at a constant value. With air miles, this isn't always true; some schemes suffer massive inflation as huge numbers of miles are earnt, and you may find that if you don't spend them for a few years, the price of the flights offered in air miles goes up. Other forms of corporate currencies include vouchers. Even if these vouchers have a nominal matching fiat currency value, they still represent a risk. For example, you should not be too keen on holding airline vouchers for any cancelled flights resulting from the Corona crisis. On an exchange rate basis, you lost fiat currency that could be spent anywhere and got in return a paper promise of a ticket of the same value, with one airline and with an expiry date. This should not have been a 1:1 exchange. You're running the risk of both flight prices increasing due to the large numbers of these vouchers in circulation, mostly with a very short validity of only a year, and also of losing the whole voucher unused if the airline goes bust. If banks go bust, then history has proved airlines definitely do regularly.

Corporate currencies aren't even a new thing. They were very popular at the beginning of the industrial revolution and into the Victorian era, commonly called *Truck*. Many employers, when taking on new employees, would pay the wages in government fiat currency value, but with their own coins instead of the government ones. These coins were then only exchangeable at a store or stores that accepted the employer's truck currency, known as *Truck shops*. What this meant in practice is that some jobs offering to pay a certain wage were often found not to be so lucrative as originally thought, because the prices at the few stores accepting the truck were often higher. Indeed, it might be hard to extricate yourself if you and your family have moved to a remote mine somewhere, and the only shop within miles accepts the mine owner's currency only.

All this should tell you is that the right to issue currency is very valuable indeed, so it's a little wonder corporations would want to be in on the act. In fact, we have seen and continue to witness a massive growth in the value of certain corporations to the extent that their market capitalisations are greater than the GDP of many nations. With that kind of power to wield, corporate currencies are bound to be offered more and more. It's not necessarily a bad thing, just as long as people know what they are and, most importantly - have options to use them or not. For example, at the beginning of September 2020, Apple's Market Capitalisation hit the same level as the whole UK FTSE-100, the leading 100 companies in the United Kingdom. These corporations are now huge.

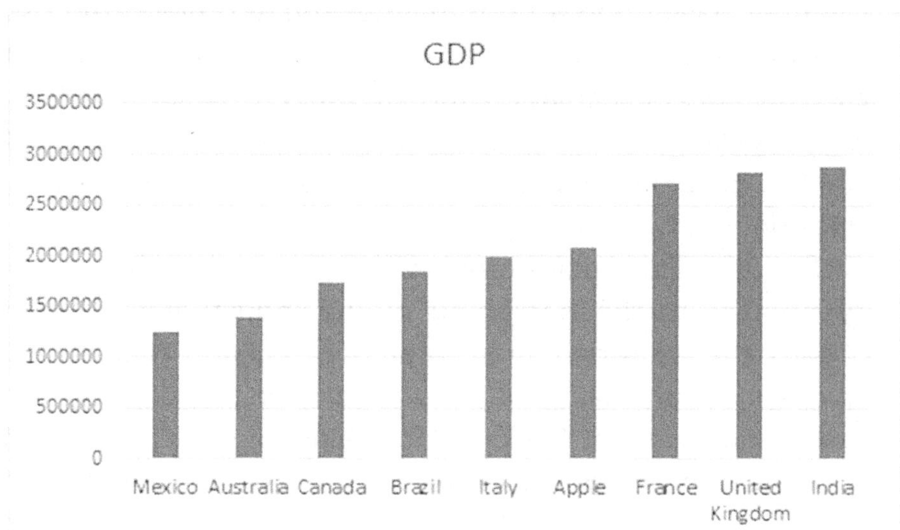


*Market Cap of Apple versus 2019 GDP for selected nations*

Now, bear in mind that just a few years ago, Apple was just above Mexico. So the trend is upward, then consider many nations are now forecasting a 2020 GDP slump of 10% or more. Apple may even be above the United Kingdom GDP before too long, perhaps even the end of this year.

## IT'S IN OUR DNA

Corporations are on the rise in terms of wealth and power. As corporate slogans go, this one is getting a lot of airtime the past couple of years, as confirmed by employees of many companies, and you may have heard it recited at your place of work too. Given what is described next, the transfer of wealth and power from governments and individuals to the corporations, it doesn't actually seem so unrealistic or safe as it might've sounded back in 2018. When it first gained traction, it seemingly tried to promote a positive corporate culture only. However, when considered alongside the Microsoft cryptocurrency patent and stories of employers implanting their employees with their access chips to get into the building, we get closer and closer every day to employers actually managing to implant their 'DNA' inside their employees. Then their values truly are in your DNA. It's now clear that for many years we have seen and still are seeing a huge wealth transfer from both individuals and governments to corporations. We may even be entering a final phase of that transfer because **The Crown** has created even more opportunities for it to happen on a much larger scale than before.

## WEALTH TRANSFER FROM GOVERNMENTS

While corporate currencies are potentially on the up, the main form of currency today, national fiat currencies, are in decline worldwide. All competing with each other seemingly to debase themselves into virtual nothingness. Corona has only exacerbated that trend. The governments only have themselves to blame, but right now, fiat currencies represent both the only medium of exchange AND the only means of stored savings for future investment for most people. It looks like a major financial storm is brewing as these national fiat currencies, with historical names like Pounds, Dollars, and Yen, continue to decline in purchasing power as more and more currency units are issued into circulation. While for some countries, the precious metal backing is declining too.

It's been made worse by the dramatic new wealth transfers that are occurring during the crisis from the government to corporate:-

- Direct corporate bailouts during the Corona crisis to businesses deemed too big or too essential to fail. Aside from the large ones such as Germany and the 9 billion Euro bailout of Lufthansa, bus companies, railways, and all kinds of businesses are seeking and obtaining funds from the government.

- Banks issuing loans to beleaguered firms in the UK, with the majority of the funds for the loans coming from the government, but the profits on the interest, sometimes as much as 30%, going to the banks themselves. In the UK, one politician, ex-Labour leader Ed Milliband even proposed that all risk of loss by the banks for non-payment of the loans should be 100% shouldered by the taxpayer. Instead of the current 80%.

- A huge extra transfer of money from the government, on your behalf, to universities and pharmaceutical companies to fund research and advance purchase millions and millions of vaccines.

Then, think about it deeper, and you will see that as governments weaken, corporations already were and are intruding more and more onto areas that were traditionally provided and run by the government. Here are a few examples:-

- Corporations increasingly running government services, with whole sections of National Health services, benefits, and even prisons now outsourced. This trend has been going on for a long time, but emergency Corona measures exacerbated it and meant, for example, that even the testing centres for

Corona in the UK are run by Deloitte, an accountancy firm instead of the National Health Service.

- The furlough scheme, where employees laid off during the Corona period are paid their salaries. The government pays the money at this moment in time but via the employer. In Germany, the furlough scheme has already been extended until the end of 2021. This is in stark contrast to all other benefit schemes, where social security is a matter between government offices and the individual citizens only.

- Companies offering advanced benefits like private healthcare, that bypass the state options. Then latterly, introducing more and more schemes like diversity, mental health awareness, and action for good days. Instead of just working for your employer on an agreed contract, they increasingly want to know more and more about you, placing themselves in your personal lifestyle.

It doesn't seem ridiculous given this encroachment that we will ultimately see a return to truck. It has already crept into many workplaces via formal systems for uprating colleagues and sometimes employees get rewards from these schemes, such as vouchers. The question of employers paying their employees in a new currency raises so many questions though - How will shops and websites price up their goods with different prices for different currencies, or will groups of large corporations band together to, say, pay their employees in, say, AmazonCoins, only redeemable at Amazon? Then there's the biggest question of all - what will happen to those on UBI, who receive their credits in devaluing government fiat do if fewer shops will take their government fiat and insist on payment in particular corporate currencies only?

There are already more subtle examples of corporate currency issuance and truck with the coming of the internet. For example, members of cashback websites that share affiliate commissions with you on things you buy may have noticed that they often offer you the opportunity to withdraw your cashback in your national currency or take vouchers to spend at retailers instead. Often, say, £10 cashback might be equal to a £10.50 retail voucher instead. No problem with that, as long as you know, you will use the voucher within the period of its validity.

In August 2019, quietly and without much fanfare, Facebook made an announcement - they introduced their own cybercurrency. Called 'Libra.' You may wonder about the name, 'Libra' - not only is it the seventh sign of the zodiac, but it is also the name for a unit of weight in ancient Rome, equivalent to 12 ounces. The 'L' sign from Libra is still used to represent the British Pound today. Will it be backed by a Pound of sterling silver, though? Probably not. In fact, Facebook wasn't totally clear on what it will be backed by, saying only "a collection of established financial assets." Actually, in that respect, it sounds a bit better-backed than the "full faith and trust of your government," but without knowing what that means, we can't be sure. What is fairly certain is that Facebook Marketplace has made massive strides in taking market share from the traditional second-hand selling publications and websites that facilitated direct person-to-person transactions and is probably hoping to develop a financial relationship in this way with its users. Depending on how Libra catches on, this could be the start of a major trend.

Now, if we do get people being paid in corporate currencies, how will it be managed? Will you need a bank account, and if so, where? Perhaps even later a situation may arise where employers electronically credit their employees via an implant with the salaried corporate currency credits every month.

## WEALTH TRANSFER FROM INDIVIDUALS

The 2020 Crown virus has also initiated a huge wealth transfer process from individuals to big corporations, not just from the government to the same corporations, as described earlier. Again, quite subtly done. Just think of some of the ways that the world has changed and how it may change even more soon:-

- Individuals and small businesses were forced to cease trading or curtail it massively. In many cases, these businesses will simply not reopen when the uncertainty is over.

- Shops and businesses relying on physical footfall that have remained open saw their earnings drop massively.

- Many individuals have lost their livelihoods, and either fell through the furlough qualification gaps, or furlough simply doesn't exist in their home countries.

This has crippled physical shops. Along with (but not limited to): Restaurants, bars, hotels, cinemas, leisure, museums, theatres, and hairdressers, to name but some. Meanwhile, shopping online was still allowed, encouraged even. It somehow didn't seem to equate that physical people are still handling the goods you were buying during the manufacturing, warehousing, and delivery processes. If your primary concern is avoiding catching a disease, that is. The fact that online shopping is now primarily done at a hardcore massively-reducing number of retail outlets should be a cause for concern. The river of consumer spending is flowing increasingly upwards to just a few of these outlets, all big corporations. As an anecdotal example, when looking for an item online recently, the search results only found it for sale at 3 places, and you can doubtless guess who two of them were - Amazon and eBay. Even a few years ago, there were a lot more online options to choose from.

Even the furlough scheme itself can be viewed as an unfair burden for small businesses and sole traders, who will have to try and do the admin themselves and get it right, lest they make damaging and costly mistakes. Compare this to the large businesses, with entire departments dedicated solely to dealing with this kind of administration, en masse, for thousands of employees at a time.

The pool of consumer choice is shrinking. When it comes to the smaller family-run businesses or even enterprising individuals, some of those who can afford to do so may have already decided this is a good time to call it a day. Others are not so lucky; they live hand-to-mouth or have only a few months of savings built up. It's not impossible that there could, in the coming months and years, be a massive tidal wave of ailing businesses and mortgage arrears on private homes, where the banks could clean up and make a lot of money. Again, the big corporations stand to make big profits from all of this uncertainty, and the government seems to be doing many things that assist them at the expense of the people who supposedly vote them in to represent them in a modern democracy. This has been referred to as 'crony capitalism,' a twisted version of the free market-capitalism that most of us are used to hearing about. In crony capitalism, companies and government representatives collude to ensure legislation passed favours them over smaller or foreign competitors. As nation-states grew and the gold and power centralised on a single location, usually the capital city, so did it become easier to lobby a few important politicians on the importance of new legislation, often sponsored by corporations and other outside interests to further an agenda. Transparency.eu estimates 30,000 lobbyists in Brussels alone, helping to ensure EU politicians notice their particular projects. Businessinsider. com reported that in 2018, the top 20 spenders on lobbying Washington, in the USA, were as follows :-

| Organisation | Spend ($m) |
| --- | --- |
| US Chamber of Commerce | 94.8 |
| National Association of Realtors | 72.8 |
| Open Society Policy Center (founded by George Soros) | 31.5 |
| Pharmaceutical Research & Manufacturers of America | 27.9 |
| American Hospital Association | 23.9 |
| Blue Cross Shield | 23.6 |
| Business Round Table | 23.1 |
| Alphabet (Google) | 21.7 |
| American Medical Association | 20.4 |
| AT&T | 18.5 |
| Boeing | 15.1 |
| Comcast | 15.0 |
| Amazon | 14.4 |
| Northrop Grumman | 14.3 |
| National Association of Broadcasters | 14.1 |
| Bayer AG | 13.4 |
| Lockheed Martin | 13.2 |
| NCTA (Internet and TV association) | 13.2 |
| Facebook | 12.6 |
| Southern Company | 12.3 |

Lobbying, in some ways, is the bypassing of individual citizens' rights by a rich minority to give their interests precedence. It certainly seems to be at odds with the one person, one vote concept, as an individual in a poor neighbourhood in a remote town could never get airtime with politicians in the same way. In the case of an organisation like 'Open Society,' they have a very international reach. Lobbyfacts.eu reports OSEPI has 16 Lobbyists working in the EU, too, and they had 56 meetings with the European Commission in the past year.

Please note that there is no accusation any of the entities in this list have done anything untoward, but it would be nice to see the documentation or even hear recordings of their meetings with politicians to help prove that citizens are still the driving force in a modern democracy.

On the subject of citizens and democracy, it's worthy of brief note that in the USA, corporations have since 2010 had in legal standing many of the same rights as a citizen. Corporate Personhood, it has been called. In the UK, in the City of London, the square mile Roman city part of England, even the Queen must ask permission from the Lord Mayor to enter, corporations even have the right to vote on democratic elections there. The majority of us think of corporations as solely an investment vehicle, a group of people investing a pool of money to make profitable financial decisions and return the dividends to the shareholders. While they are still that, there seems to be a much darker trend emerging with major implications if it comes to pass.

Another factor in **The Crown** has been the massive switch from working in a centralised office location to working from home for those still with employment. Even now, many large organisations have not returned to the office to work, or are even announcing that they plan to introduce new working practices. It has been dressed up as something beneficial for all parties - employers and employees, but look beneath the surface, and it may not be so clear;

Employees were expected in many cases to accept working from home during the crisis, providing office space, office facilities, and IT/telecommunications facilities that the employer previously had to offer. Most commonly, without being remunerated. Most employees accepted - due to the crisis, even if their contracts did not state homeworking or specifically stated against homeworking. Considering that a survey in 2020 suggested an office space, per average worker, costs $10,000, this is a massive saving for corporations if they can get employees to agree to working from home and shouldering these costs personally, permanently. We can also only wonder what medical issues, like depression, back, and eye problems, might become apparent later due to this. Or what social problems may occur.

Will this also lead to the erosion of nation-states, as people migrate to where taxes are lowest and work from there instead? Many countries have rules on work carried out in their country being taxable, even if the worker is not a resident there. A tax minefield has opened up, and the natural order of things may be that if an office worker can retain the first-world salary, but spend at least part of the year in holiday destinations, or a cheaper country where tax rates are lower, they may decide to do so. The next chapter, **50 percent a slave**, looks at the decline of the nation-state in more detail. Little could speed it up quicker than an exodus of their most productive citizens, who traditionally bear the heaviest tax load on their shoulders. How a society can collapse and how the government responds when the most productive members cease to participate was covered in the novel 'Atlas Shrugged' by Ayn Rand. Like Marmite, this book is either loved or loathed by readers, but its view of a dystopian 1950s America in slow-motion decline is not too similar to now, in some ways.

## SUMMARY

The major principle of modern corporations was that they were originally formed with the sole aim of providing goods and services in return for payment. The counterpart of the transaction should always have the free choice of purchasing or not purchasing those goods or services - without penalty. The payment method itself should also be something mutually agreed upon in any transaction - person-to-person or person-to-company. This is all in danger of changing. Being paid in truck is one possibility. Going back to the point earlier made about governments dealing more and more with corporations, supposedly on your behalf, some of that transactional freedom of choice is eroded - you, the private individual, no longer got to choose whether to participate in the transaction or not. The argument about being able to vote them out in 4-5 years through the democratic process is a rather moot one, considering it'll be far too late by then. A third party decided how your money got distributed, and worse, they usually do so without the same regard for the value that most of us do when deciding whether or not to participate in a transaction voluntarily.

In addition to selling services to governments, corporations now seem to have more say with governments through lobbying to get legislation written that favours them over smaller competitors. If the government does try to stand up to it, they could just threaten to walk away completely from even doing business in a particular jurisdiction or to transfer employees and facilities elsewhere. The UK Prime Minister even has regular conference calls nowadays with FTSE-100 leaders. Corporations also now have more control over individuals. Fewer and fewer people are self-employed, and Corona has speeded that process up. Even IR35, a UK scheme to ensure small businesses pay their 'fair share of tax,' has the net effect of pushing more independent freelancers into becoming treated as employees instead. Individual consumer choice is also being eroded. Sometimes now a big corporation is the sole producer or sole seller of certain items. None of this would be bad, of course, if it were based on fair competition. The question being, is it?

It's clear why multinational corporations might be interested in introducing their own currencies across the territories they operate in and sidestepping national governments next. These new currencies would still be as a medium of exchange. Little difference whether a corporation issues it or a government. No-one should be thinking of having their life savings in one online shopping website's vouchers or air miles, but there again, when you really think about it, it should get you wondering whether the same rule applies to have your life savings in one government's fiat currency. If you do ever receive payment in a corporate currency, then the next question is, what is backing it? If the corporate cybercurrency is gold-backed, at a fixed ratio to currency units in circulation, then that increases the intrinsic value of the currency. However, there's every reason to believe that exactly as with government-issued fiat, too many currency units will be issued eventually, and there will likely be no or very little underlying precious metal behind each unit.

Corporate currencies may have a place, and indeed, the more competing currencies out there in a genuine free market, the greater our personal freedom would be, but in some ways, they suggest an extremely dystopian Bladerunner-type future, where corporations own and run everything, indeed becoming the new countries themselves. It's possible that corporate currencies may even usurp government currencies, and with that, the government currencies may actually simply disappear. Common people could lose everything - their savings, their ability even to live and survive. Where the gold and silver currently held in governmental vaults will end up is, right now, anyone's guess. You may remember in The Rise and Fall of Empires; it was said that many people think China is the next big empire. No, plenty things are going on in the world to suggest that we may be experiencing one of the biggest wealth transfers in human history from governments and individuals to corporations, and the next big empire may just as easily be Microsoft, Alphabet (Google), Apple, Amazon, Tencent or Alibaba.

Next, we cover individual citizens and their relationship with the government.

# 50 PERCENT A SLAVE

"You choose your leaders and place your trust
As their lies put you down and their
promises rust."

— The Jam, Going Underground 1980

An alternative working title for this chapter was "Fiat Finito." This is not the latest car model by the Italian manufacturer, but a suggestion we may well be living through the end of governmental fiat currency. To put it in perspective, many national currencies have declined to less than 1% of their original value. In other words, 99% of the decline has already happened, and we are now living through the era of the final 1%.

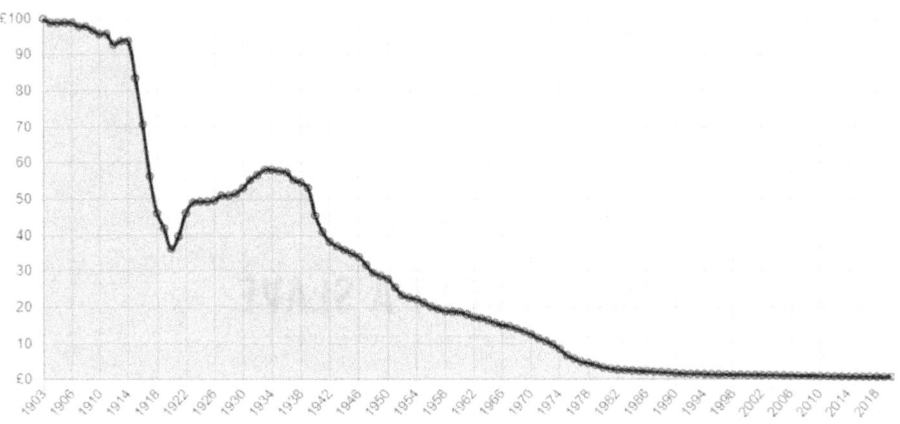

*(Chart showing decline of GBP purchasing power since gold standard era)*

The **Barbarous relic versus the Barbarous Privilege** again and what a barbarous privilege it turned out to be, the right to dictate to the entire population that they must use one particular means of exchange and no other. That in itself is a form of slavery, a major curtailment of freedom that cannot be measured. The barbarous privilege has left us all in a position where in most developed economies, citizens are now paying up to 50% of their income in taxes, and it continues to rise. Even with 50%, this fails to consider the stealth taxes on the earnt fiat currency income through inflation.

Tax Wedge in OECD Countries 2019

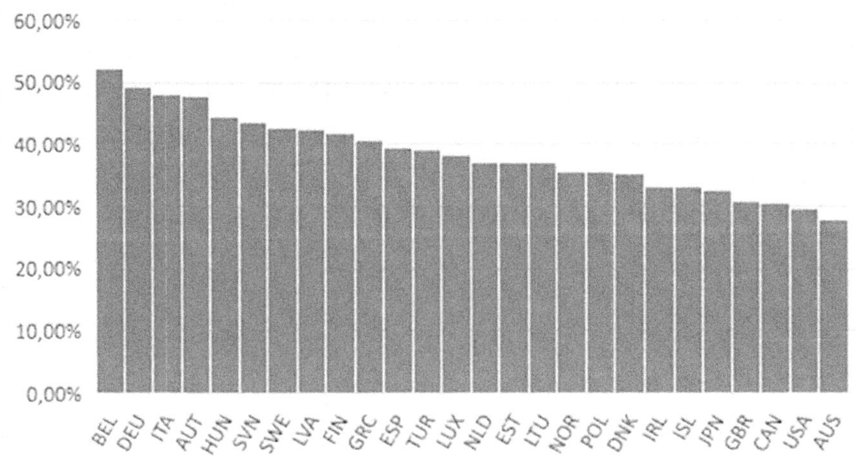

*Data Source: OECD*

Ultimately, what country you live in, or what government rules over you only defines the extent to which you are a slave and the Western world, even official statistics say it's getting up to around *Fifty Percent*. In this context, the clothes you are wearing, the smartphone in your hand-assembled by subsistence-level workers in faraway countries, the commodities themselves mined by young children in squalid conditions may sometimes be much closer to being a 100% slave than you probably are, but you are *still a slave*. You may disagree but think about this - what if you decided to quit your job and lead a self-sufficient lifestyle in the home that you own, growing your own vegetables and trying to live outside of the financial system. You would fail extremely quickly because immediately there are still taxes to be paid - for example, property taxes - and these taxes are all denominated in the governmental fiat currency. Simply put, to pay those taxes, you must now have earnings or savings in the same currency. You don't have a choice in the matter, except to move to another country, but even that is a moot point since the new country will probably desire its pound of flesh in much the same manner.

Not only this, but **Fractional Reserve Banking** explained how debts with interest are created as multiples of the same deposit. Since fiat currency is no longer linked to gold, debts generally have risen massively. Be it Government or personal, these debts can also be viewed as chains. Even just to stay alive as a hamster on the wheel, you must earn enough in fiat currency to pay the taxes on the governmental debt, as well as repayments on your own debt for a place to live. All this before you can even start to enjoy any of the fruits of your labour at all.

## CORONA CRISIS

The Corona crisis seems to have, temporarily at least, increased trust in these governments and state media as people consider them to be benevolently protecting them. Yet many of the welfare state schemes described in **Social Insecurity**, to supposedly protect people and look after them in their time of need, have completely collapsed. For example, in the UK during 2020, many hospitals switched to emergency services only, cleared out patients, and closed down entire departments that were deemed non-essential. This has resulted in backlogs of two years or more. To say little of the as yet largely unknown increased casualty lists from undiagnosed severe illnesses like cancer and heart disease that aren't being identified sooner to give people a chance of survival. Yet, taxes continue to rise, and people are continuously getting less while paying more. More and more of the tax you pay goes to fund the interest on the debts built up by the government, less and less goes to fund anything useful. As a citizen, were you given a choice in taking out those debts or not?

That taxes will rise to pay for the Corona crisis in some way or other is a given. However, with income tax straining and sales taxes in the European Union as high as 25%, there is not so much scope to increase these much more. Then, fiat currency inflation is already high. This leaves a need for more inventive ways to extract the pound of flesh from the citizenry.

In the book "Animal Farm" by George Orwell, there's a horse named Boxer. Boxer works hard all his life, but when the time comes that he is worn out, instead of thanking him for his loyalty and putting him out to pasture, the two pigs in charge sell him off to the glue factory. On the same vein, the next logical but an extremely unpleasant step is that citizens may turn from being milk cows into prime beef, as in desperation, the grabbing of assets becomes real. That's ridiculous, you may say - but it's already happened. Also, do you remember what Christine Lagarde said in **The Crown**, about a job is more important than savings? Here are some examples:-

- In 2013, in Cyprus, a new financial crisis occurred. Unlike 2008-09, instead of government (via the taxpayer, of course) funds bailing out the banks, customers of those banks had funds forcibly confiscated from their accounts to fund the banks. This was termed a bail-in, instead of a bail-out.

- In 2014, the UK took over the Post Office workers pension scheme and the £30bn of assets contained within it, against a paper, non-asset backed promise to pay postal workers pensions in the future.

- In 2020, the UK government announced that they would confiscate the funds of all dormant bank accounts, "...To support Covid-19 causes..."

These are but 3 examples. There are probably many more similar accounting tricks being carried out across the world. The main point is - your assets and savings are under attack. Not just by the ravages of inflation, that is no longer enough. The next -ation is confiscation. Whether it's your pension savings or bank savings, there are already real-life examples. Cyprus may have been a small-world testbed before the policies are implemented in other larger nations. It's also in the EU, and organising the 2014 bailout was assisted by the ECB, which Lagarde now heads.

Even in the UK amid the Corona crisis, carefully-placed media articles appeared saying that a wealth tax may be necessary, but that (paraphrased) "...If it did happen and were done correctly, the economy would not suffer". If you have read Edward Bernays's book from 1928, "Propaganda," you will be aware that such media stories are often carefully placed to drive or test public opinion. If you have not read this book, then it is recommended that you do so. Apparently, Goebbels, one of Hitler's henchmen, was a big fan.

> "Whatever of social importance is done today, whether in politics, finance, manufacture, agriculture, charity, education, or other fields, must be done with the help of propaganda."
>
> — *Edward L. Bernays, Propaganda*

## THE DEATH OF NATIONS

National government is in decline. It's been a great tool to control populations and bring about many group activities that would otherwise not have been possible. Like causing the death of millions and the transfer of wealth and assets from the many to the few through many schemes. Not the least of which has been the theme of this book - the lie that they will look after your wealth safely and securely, allowing you to use representative currency units that you can then exchange for the requisite amount of gold and silver. Try taking your £1 coin to the bank of England and ask for your one pound in weight of sterling silver and see how far you get, if you remain in any doubt.

The final part of this act in the history of mankind - nation-states are, after all, a fairly recent invention, even countries we think of as well-established, like Germany and Italy, were but a patchwork of small independent countries before the 1870s, may yet be quite a major one. Even the United Kingdom has only existed in the current form since 1920 when Southern Ireland seceded, and going back to 1707, Scotland and England were separate nations.

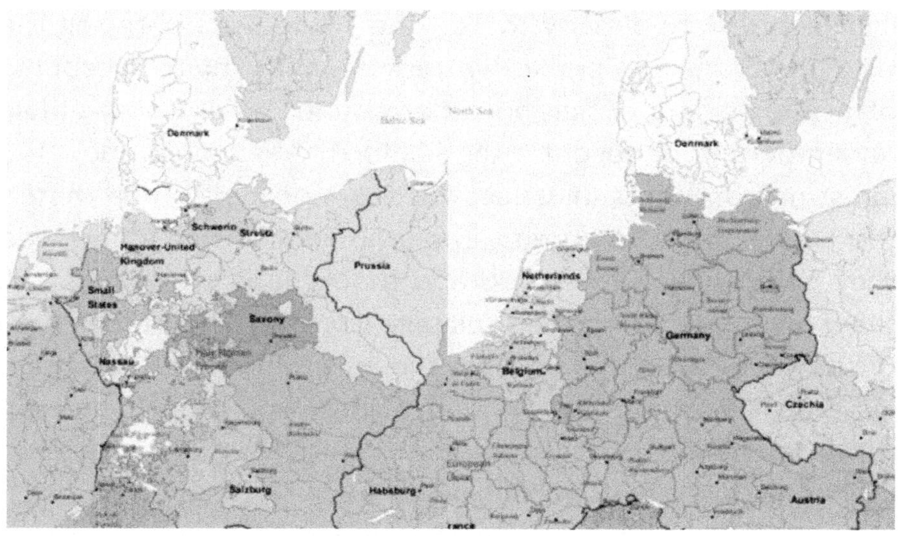

*(Chart: Germany 1800 versus present day*

Countries have grown into huge entities, with massive power over millions, billions even of people and more worryingly still, access to huge swathes of military hardware and technology to do immense harm in the wrong hands. Perhaps the last act will also be a geopolitical crescendo, culminating in some kind of war. Just like the last kick of a dying horse, you probably won't want to be in the way if or when it happens, and given the title of this chapter, what is mandatory participation in a war you don't want to fight but an increase in the percentage you are a slave to something a lot closer to 100%? Be it your life, your children's lives, or forced confiscation of your savings to help pay for it.

It's not beyond the realms of possibility. In fact, **The Rise and Fall of Empires** highlighted that almost every new empire clashes with the old at some point, and the further in time you travel from the last huge conflict, the more people seem to forget the ingrained memory of the true horrors of war that got passed down from the generations that last experienced it. The clues are already there - the Trade wars between the USA and China, the public Twitter comments by the accounts of world leaders criticising other countries for being unfair, undemocratic, or despotic, the slanted media stories about the latest human rights injustices in Russia or Syria. Then there's the jingoism of the current imperial number one, convinced they could police the world and mould it in their image, all the while celebrating their military victories and heroes with gusto. All of these are grist for the mill, things to think about, like pieces of a massive geopolitical jigsaw puzzle that you can only assemble as best you can and guess at what's contained in the missing pieces you'll never find.

## THE LOSS OF FREEDOM

In **The Barbarous Relic versus the barbarous privilege**, we looked at the economic theories of John Maynard Keynes and how they were adopted across the world in the 1930s, before World War Two. Look at the similarities now. The Crown virus, Covid-19, has led to a tidal wave of newly-created currency across the world for bailouts, furlough, and extra government spending. If the economic hardships and Keynesian years in the 1930s in some way contributed to the rise of extreme government policies and ideologies then, could it perhaps happen again? Germany was a very developed first world country that somehow turned to extreme fascism while government spending on infrastructure projects like motorways and the military was huge. Fascism may not be dead - move into the modern era, and the Corona crisis has introduced many policies that could be used to subvert human rights and democratic actions of citizens in the future. Look at these three new policies in the UK, for example, all introduced in the Corona wake, in May 2020:-

- It's now illegal to gather in groups of more than ten people. Later reduced to six, with '...Six feet apart or six feet under', completing the new tagline. Enforced by COVID-19 marshalls, starting September 2020

- One doctor and one nurse can now declare you ill under the mental health act and have you detained indefinitely without trial.

- People can be "evacuated" from their homes by force, and property can now be demolished by government order.

With any law passed, the wisest way to look at it is - how would this law be implemented if the worst type of dictator was in charge? Chances are that someday they might be, just as they were in 1930s Germany when Hitler and his cronies took control. The UK is not alone in implementing policies of this type - just examine the newly introduced laws in the country where you live and ask yourself the same questions. Many people have stated that if they were in Germany in the 1930s and saw the erosion of human rights or the attacks on Jews, they "would've done something." Yet, when Corona happened, the majority took it without protest, and indeed, police telephones and hotlines logged plenty of calls from members of the public concerned about others having family gatherings or taking more than one walk a day outside.

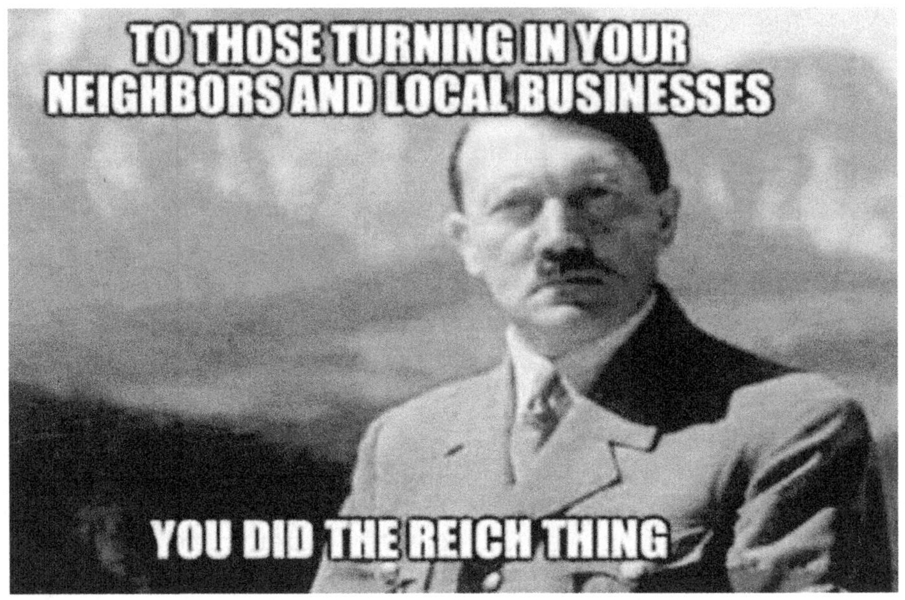


*Some saw the relevance after New York introduced a 'snitch' hotline*

"Of course, the people don't want war. But after all, it's the leaders of the country who determine the policy, and it's always a simple matter to drag the people along whether it's a democracy, a fascist dictatorship, or a parliament, or a communist dictatorship. Voice or no voice, the people can always be brought to the bidding of the leaders. That is easy. All you have to do is tell them they are being attacked, and denounce the pacifists for lack of patriotism, and exposing the country to greater danger."

— Herman Goering at the Nuremberg trials

Germany, in the 1930s, gives another great example of wealth confiscation in the way that property was grabbed, often literally, from citizens. The images of Jews being dragged off trains and thoroughly searched, any hidden gold or currency being confiscated may well be repeated except this time it won't necessarily be the Jews, but some other subset of the population that is viewed as the *untermenschen* - old people, those unwilling to take the vaccine, or those unwilling to surrender their wealth to the state, perhaps? Whereas again, you might have thought citizens would express their disgust at this ill-treatment of a fellow human. Douglas Reed, in his 1938 classic "Insanity Fair," which predicted the invasion of Czechoslovakia and World War 2, was present and described it well. He talks of the cheering and general support for such moves, as he travels out of Austria during the *Anschluss*, annexation by Germany - and even has some of his own currency confiscated. If you think you're above this, think again and refer once more to Edward Bernays 1928 classic "Propaganda." Ways can always be found to mould public opinion in the desired way so that people think 'they deserve it.' If the first casualty in a war is the truth, then the second may well be justice.

> "The conscious and intelligent manipulation of the organized habits and opinions of the masses is an important element in a democratic society. Those who manipulate this unseen mechanism of society constitute an invisible government which is the true ruling power of our country."
>
> — Edward L. Bernays, Propaganda

## THE ROAD TO FASCISM

In **The Road to from Democracy to Corporatocracy**, we looked at a possible corporate takeover of the world. This possibility is not incompatible with a rise in fascism. Again, Nazi Germany provides us with a great example of how businesses can co-exist and prosper in such an environment, a marriage between government and big business. For example:-

- AG Farben, a massive chemical conglomerate, supplied the military, Manufactured Zyklon B, the nerve gas, and was a large donor to the Nazi party. While you may not recognise the name, that's because, after World War 2, they divided into separate entities that you may recognise: BASF, Bayer, Agfa, and Sanofi. As an aside, they even invented Fanta in this period, the well-known Orange flavoured soda, to overcome a shortage of Coca-Cola.

- Industrial conglomerates like Krupp manufactured military hardware.

- Porsche produced tanks, including the famous *Tiger* and the not-so-successful *Elefant*, a design failure with a fixed gun that pointed only in one direction and no machine gun.

- Hugo Boss designed and manufactured uniforms.

- Dr Oetker supplied the army provisions.

Whether such a marriage is a desirable outcome for the people themselves is a separate matter to consider and one we may have to face in the coming years. As is the question of if, whether it does go that way, war and virtual 100% slavery is the outcome. There has rarely been a time to be more alert to the actions of the entities around you then right now in August 2020. Not only are your financial savings in extreme danger, but your human rights are eroded. What is the word 'lockdown anyway,' but a word to refer to prisoners being confined to their cells? Did you know you were a prisoner in the first place?

The 1930-40s, in both Germany and Italy, show that government can carry on being the acceptable face of 'democracy,' so that the people feel invested and that they have a say, but behind the scenes, freedom is limited, human decency to each other is corroded, and the country is run ultimately for the benefit of the corporations. At its height, in 1943, IG Farben, the German chemical manufacturer, employed an estimated and staggering 330,000 people. From a top-level economics point of view, you could argue Germany enjoyed full employment, huge productivity gains, and a deluge of new inventions. Just ignore the human cost, as many of those employees were, in fact, forced labour and fast forward 2 years to 1945 and see how well the economy was doing.

> "Not everything that counts can be counted, and not everything that can be counted counts."
>
> — Albert Einstein.

1933-45 also proves that this marriage can exist for years before it falls apart and, on the surface, can actually look like an economic success story to the rest of the world. It's not so often mentioned, but the Berlin Olympics of 1936 were Germany's big presentation to the world of its new economic prowess and power; Hitler was Time Magazine's Man of the Year in 1938, and he even makes an edited cameo appearance in the 1940 epic, "Citizen Kane", alongside Kane himself - the gist of the scene being that Kane is a big player on the world stage and can sit alongside a great leader - at this point, despite the invasions of Czechoslovakia and Poland, Hitler was still believed by many worldwide to be a genius who had revived an ailing country and not a despotic dictator, already responsible for the deaths of many by 1940.

Any future decline and fragmentation of nation-states do not necessarily mean a decline into anarchy. Germany may again be the greatest example of this. Compare the 1933 Germany to The 1923 version, when a destitute country that had just been bankrupted by a 4-year war suffered that huge hyperinflation that destroyed society and left much of the middle class with no savings. It's perhaps an example of when an ailing nation-state is lifted from its grave and used as a puppet on a string by higher powers. For example, foreign banking corporations, including familiar US family names from today, certainly played a part in refinancing the country back to apparent prosperity and then war. As long as the democratic illusion exists, but gets gradually eroded, people seem more amenable to participate in it. "Insanity Fair" describes much of the rise of Nazism close-up, reporting on the sham trials and gradual erosion of freedom there in the 1930s. It's interesting that in the modern world, the largest supranational bloc, The European Union, contains modern Germany as its largest country. Also that this bloc now has its own currency, flag, and national anthem - along with lawmakers, elections, courts, and collection of tribute from the countries within it. Citizens of declining nation-states within this bloc are being gradually led towards a new super-state most of them are blithely unaware of.

When the United Kingdom tried to leave, it took 4 years before some kind of treaty was signed that, on the surface, sounded like it was leaving to appease the democratic aspect of the population. Yet, underneath it moved the negotiations another year forward and left the UK within the bloc, but now with no say while still sending massive tribute and receiving much less back in return, all to be spent on favoured EU interests. That a 2018 survey found the UK has nine of the ten most impoverished regions of Northern Europe is not a coincidence. It's also a major sign of weakening nation-states -

especially ex-imperial powers with little to no gold left, having to accept rules from someone else.

> "Europe's nations should be guided towards the superstate without their people understanding what is happening. This can be accomplished by successive steps, each disguised as having an economic purpose, but which will eventually and irreversibly lead to federation."
>
> — Jean Monnet, one of the founders of the European Union

From a military point of view, this new supranational bloc is creeping its borders further and further east. Absorbing Poland, the Baltic states, and perhaps in the not-too-distant future, western Ukraine. It also announced in 2018 that it needed to form an army, something it had denied for years. Certainly, the region has a major recent history of conflict; just go back to 75 years ago. Unless something changes, this looks like a potential future flashpoint.

Ultimately, whatever form any future war took, you can be assured it probably won't be the same as the last two world wars, where there were massed human armies on both sides, embroiled in fights to the death at previously unknown places with names like The Somme, Verdun or Kursk. Certainly, these wars will involve a whole new front line, which brings us nicely to the next big future thing to consider - *technology.*

# DATA IS THE NEW OIL

"As new technologies seem to race towards us from the far horizon, we strain our eyes as they come, to make out whether they are for good or bad, friends or foes."

— Boris Johnson, August 2019

In August 2019, Boris Johnson, the UK Prime Minister, made an unusual speech at the United Nations about the march of technology, referencing Prometheus from Greek Mythology. Many press commentators believed the Prometheus reference to be about Brexit, the U.K.'s ailing attempt to exit cleanly from the European Union. You should not be so sure. Johnson is an expert on Greek Mythology, so he knows exactly what Prometheus represents to mankind.

For the uninitiated, Prometheus was one of the Titans, the gods who created mankind. Unknown to the other gods, he gifted mankind fire so that civilisation could progress. Zeus was not too happy about this and had Prometheus chained to a mountain, where every day, a bird would fly down and peck out his liver, leaving him in agonising pain, we assume.

The liver would heal, and then the process would repeat every day for eternity. Nice. Again, Hollywood has partly prepared us for this by actually creating a film of the same name, "Prometheus" in 2012.

Given that story, an alternative take on his Prometheus references would be that mankind has been gifted a new fire, technology, and whether the human race advances or even destroys itself depends on what it does with that fire.

## THE TECHNOLOGY ERA

Just as the industrial era usurped the agricultural era, we are witnessing the death of the industrial era and the start of the information technology era, the data age. The Industrial era started approximately in the 1760s with the exploitation of coal and some new inventions such as James Watt's Steam engine and James Hargreaves's Spinning Jenny, meaning previously home-manufactured, cottage-industry wares could now be mass-produced and fell dramatically in price. The era really took off in the UK with what can be seen now as a major switch in policy to get the country even more focused on manufacturing instead of agriculture, when the Corn Laws were repealed in the 1840s. This meant cheaper and cheaper agricultural imports undermined local farmers, leading to the displacement of agricultural workers to the cities and the colonies where they could earn more money - or, perhaps, for many, even just earn some money at all.

Ultimately, it could be viewed that they were thought of as workers still working on jobs considered to be part of the previous era, who then need to be "freed up," along with their resources and those of the farmers they worked for. Of course, there'll always be a need for manufactured goods, just as there is still a need for food, but these industries only employ a fraction of the numbers they traditionally needed before.

Many agricultural and industrial needs are now exposed to future technological changes, and it's most certainly a subject worthy of closer examination. Even baby milk itself may be changing, with a fund co-founded by Bill Gates, Jeff Bezos (Amazon), Zuckerberg (Facebook), and Richard Branson, just announcing an investment in a company called BIQMILQ, which plans to produce new artificial breast milk from cells. If the first food we eat as babies is capable of modification, think how far it could go elsewhere.

Even the World Economic Forum openly refers to 2020 now as "The Great Economic Reset" on their official website. How interesting that what caused the pressing of that reset button, which as a metaphor conjures up images of a crashed PC in an ailing state needing a reboot and possibly a hard-drive clearout to get it working better, was again, the Crown virus. Simply put, people would never have accepted losing their jobs, livelihoods, and personal freedoms unless they were told they were under attack and necessary for the greater good. While history can again be sparse in providing us with written details of the trials and tribulations of ordinary people, you can guess it wasn't all upwards for everyone in the move from the agricultural age to the industrial age. There are certainly some alludations to the darker side of the industrial revolution in novels by Charles Dickens, Jane Austen, and Elizabeth Gaskell, for example. Even the move from the Stone age to the Bronze age provides some interesting examples of job losses and dying skills - Archaeologists often find stone axes of increasing ornateness from the period when bronze axes began to appear - the older craftsmen, working with the older technology, tried harder to save their livelihoods and compete with the new technology, is the suggested main reason. Modern government seems determined to mandate that that isn't even a choice.

## WINNERS AND LOSERS

You don't need to be particularly insightful to see who some of the real winners of this Corona crisis are. While traditional shops, pubs, and restaurants are bad, think about this:-

- Shopping online, especially at larger retailers, is unaffected and fine.

- Everyone that can is switching to digital means of communication and work

- People are transacting and communicating online more.

- There's a major push for vaccines and a COVID-19 health passport.

From these items, you can only imagine how much extra data companies like Amazon, Microsoft, Facebook, and Google have been able to gather lately. It's a goldmine. Figuratively speaking.

Not only has the gathering of data increased massively, but in recent years the storage location of the data itself has changed dramatically. Before the internet, all data was stored on floppy disks of varying sizes - 8", then $5\frac{1}{4}$", then $3\frac{1}{2}$", with increasing storage levels as the technology improved. This data could not be shared except amongst those physically able to pass on the disk to computers that had the correct drive to read the data. It became possible as computers were networked up together to store data on network drives where it could be shared. Alongside this, computers themselves began to have hard disks of increasing speed and size so that files could be stored on the computer itself. Nowadays, many organisations have moved on from even hosting the software themselves on their own hardware - they use something called the Cloud to run important business systems.

"There's no such thing as the cloud, just someone else's computer."

— Various sources

*Disclaimer - I know some tech people will disagree with me and say it's just software, as most servers now are virtual: i.e., just software partitioned logically, so hundreds of servers can be running on the same machine. Even so, there still needs to be a physical computer behind it somewhere.*

Most of us use the cloud daily without even realising it. Many of the mainstream websites you use for banking, shopping, or, indeed watch TV on demand are run in the cloud. Netflix even uses Amazon Workspaces as its cloud solution. Amazon is actually doing very well in providing cloud services, with huge business-critical IT systems and large databases full of important corporate data now running on Amazon servers. Yes, Amazon is not just about shopping online.

Microsoft introduced new chat and meeting software, 'Teams' in the year before the crisis. That's when it appeared for most on their PCs, often automatically, without even a download option beforehand. Designed to take over from Skype, Teams has already established itself as the first choice chat, messenger, and video conferencing software in many commercial organisations. It makes it easy to share files and video the calls for future reference. There is, however, one major difference with it compared to much other software of the same type that has gone before - all of these files being shared are stored on remote Microsoft servers.

Facebook and Google also have their own messaging and video chat services, all being well-used during the lockdown, for both business and personal use. In addition to this, there are the well-established and heavily-used email services provided by Microsoft and Google. All in all, a lot of data is capable of being harvested, even if some of it is not being actually harvested right now, it is potentially sitting there, stored for later exploitation. YouTube is already using AI-style robots that can scan videos for inappropriate images or keywords and censor accordingly.

Meanwhile, Amazon and Google have gone one step further with devices you put in your home, like Alexa, and talk to. Asking questions or assigning tasks to do, like find the solution to something or play music. There are plenty of stories out there of these devices mishearing their owner and doing something amusingly inappropriate, like order a pizza or purchase on Amazon automatically. This obviously seems something of a joke, but worse still, these devices can actually record your conversations. Ask yourself, where is that data being stored, and how may it be used in the future?

All in all, an incredible amount of data has been collected during the Corona crisis. Way, way over what would normally be collected if the crisis had not occurred. There are millions more online calls and chats between employees occurring that would, up until very recently, have occurred in person either formally or informally at the coffee machine or someone's desk at work. Then add in the increased socialising and family conversations that have taken, and continue to take place via technology instead of in-person since March.

Meanwhile, Bill Gates continues to push for increased vaccinations as a solution to the Corona crisis. Alongside this, Microsoft is a founding partner of something called ID2020, working together with GAVI and Accenture. This may have struggled to gain traction had it not been for the Corona crisis. ID 2020 is intended to be a digital certificate of your health and identity that you carry around in your phone and can potentially be scanned without even leaving your pocket. That GAVI, the Global Alliance for Vaccine and Immunisation, funded by the Bill and Melinda Gates Foundation, is one of the main partners alongside Microsoft indicates what kind of data is intended to be part of the ID.

## NET RESULT

One scary possible net result of all this data gathering has also been covered in a Hollywood blockbuster - *Terminator*. You may recall that the story is one of time travel from a future war between humanity and the machines, but do you remember the backstory to it? *Skynet,* an AI computer system was built that people plugged their devices into, gifting their data and allowing the system to gather it from every human interaction with the internet, data-mining on an extreme scale. Something that seemed like sci-fi nonsense back in 1984, but now seems slightly more realistic and will doubtless become even closer to potential reality as the years progress, and technological prowess grows. The net outcome of all the data mining? Skynet worked out within 24 hours that humanity was a weak link and needed to be destroyed.

We are on the verge – well, it's already started – of a huge struggle between ethics and technology. When it comes to handing over data online, there have been no real discussions about it. Few people are even asking about whether someone's voice or video image is actually ok to be stored in the cloud, yet these are unique characteristics of us that could be misused by someone someday. Unfortunately, given the response of many to the recent loss of freedom with Corona, It's hard to trust in ethics from many people, businesses, and government in short to medium term.

## CENSORSHIP

If Data is indeed the new oil, then a lack of data may be the new method of starvation, control, and censorship. Germany, in the 1930s, under National Socialism, had its own major burning of the books. Publications considered to be subversive, or presenting thoughts and ideas counter to the prevailing group-think logic of the time were put in piles and publicly burnt. Think also of the United Kingdom and how the novel "Lady Chatterley's Lover" was not publicly available in uncensored form until 1960. How we laugh now at such times, we're free, aren't we?

Maybe not.

Fast forward to now, 2020, and look at the censorship of Literature, Film, and TV after the George Floyd death in the USA. In the aftermath, TV channels decided entire films and shows were no longer suitable for broadcasting anymore, and whole scenes were cut from popular shows. Oscar-winning 'Gone with the Wind', from 1939, was an early victim for its US Civil War setting. It got so bad in the UK that even the famous "Don't mention the war" scene by John Cleese, from the late-70s TV comedy show "Fawlty Towers" got cut. If you don't have the DVD to refer to, in many cases, you won't even know the show has been edited, which suggests that having everything available online only is also a major risk - the oh so elegant streaming solution you rely on as you clear out the physical DVDs and music CDs and switch to online streaming may yet work against you in the long term. The names of the Amazon devices for reading books digitally even hint at burning of the physical books, with the first one called "Kindle" to begin the flame and the second one called "Fire." So, ask yourself this question - if a book, piece of music, or film is no longer available online and no physical copies exist, does it still exist, or has it been burnt, just as the Germans did almost 90 years ago? Books like '1984' by George Orwell and 'Fahrenheit 451' can help understand potential censorship. '1984' especially seems eerily prescient of much that has occurred in the last 20-30 years.

It doesn't end there. Entire channels and Facebook groups are being deleted daily. Often the media being deleted isn't even illegal but deemed by YouTube or Facebook to be unsuitable. For example, Europe's largest independent radio show 'Richie Allen' received three YouTube strikes in quick succession in 2017, and the whole channel was deleted without clear reasons why. The final strike was for an interview with someone who believed the school shooting at Sandy Hook in Connecticut in 2013 was fake. This, despite Allen interviewing with journalistic integrity, asking relevant questions to try and establish why the interviewee believed it to be so. Deleting content that is not illegal is certainly an ethical question will grow and grow in the future. If people ever realise it is happening.

## FEEDING THE MACHINE

While Data may seem slightly off-topic in a book about gold, this was to explain where the world is going, where the wealth is migrating to, and the importance of our data in feeding that machine. In other words, who wins the data war probably also gets the gold. To the victor, the spoils.

To look at it another way, the technology era is data-driven. Mankind already learnt how to build machines in the industrial era. Lots of them, in all shapes and sizes, then utilised them to perform manual tasks. Certainly, the machines will get more complex, but the big difference in the technology era that will make new machines closer to sentient beings is the data that is gathered and how that data can be utilised. Humans themselves are great examples of this. When a baby is born, it's, to a large extent, a blank slate. For sure, it has inherited much in its genes, perhaps more than science has yet discovered, but the next step is data-gathering. From the sound of its parents and grandparents, to the tastes, touch, scents, and sights, any human is constantly gathering data. In the same vein, the more data IT systems can collect, query, and use effectively; the more powerful the machines will get in the future.

A logical extension is that the more ways you can find to gather data, the more data you have available to use. Whereas once data-gathering was quite hard, the devices are now capable of not only harvesting government and corporate databases of our life data, but they're also now gathering photographic data - how many cameras of different types are out there recording our daily lives? Then, the new devices we bring into our homes, the Smart TVs, Smartphones, and Alexas, all have the power to gather sounds and videos of us inside our personal spaces. Meanwhile, smart meters gather detailed analysis of our power and water usage, to the extent when the suppliers can identify the exact points you went to the toilet or had a cup of tea. In the UK, already the country with the most cameras monitoring its population, recent court cases have highlighted that police gather facial recognition data from innocent people walking the streets, going about their daily business. One man in London even got fined after pulling his top up to hide his face as he walked past the camera. In Cardiff, a judge ruled facial data gathering was legal, but a recent appeal decided otherwise. How this goes in the future is anyone's guess.

Hollywood already explored this in the 2011 TV series, "Person of Interest." In this series, an omnipresent computer system called 'The Machine' gathers data from almost all computer systems - governmental, banks, security systems, motorway cameras, you name it and builds up profiles of everyone. This is for government surveillance, including crime. The inventor has a back door where he gets notifications of people involved, either wittingly or unwittingly, in a crime yet to come and can change the outcome. The message, perhaps, is that while the machine is bad, it can have a good side. The series gets much darker in later episodes, as the inventor becomes a target for other parties.

## POWER

What should be clear from all this is that power usage is probably going to rise significantly, more so than most of us realise. The multitude of new IT systems, the increased data, the mining and manufacturing of metals, alloys, and plastics to manufacture all this new technology. They are all going to consume a lot of power. Even if humans themselves #StayAtHome and drive their cars less.

For many years, gold and Oil actually maintained a near 10:1 ratio relationship.

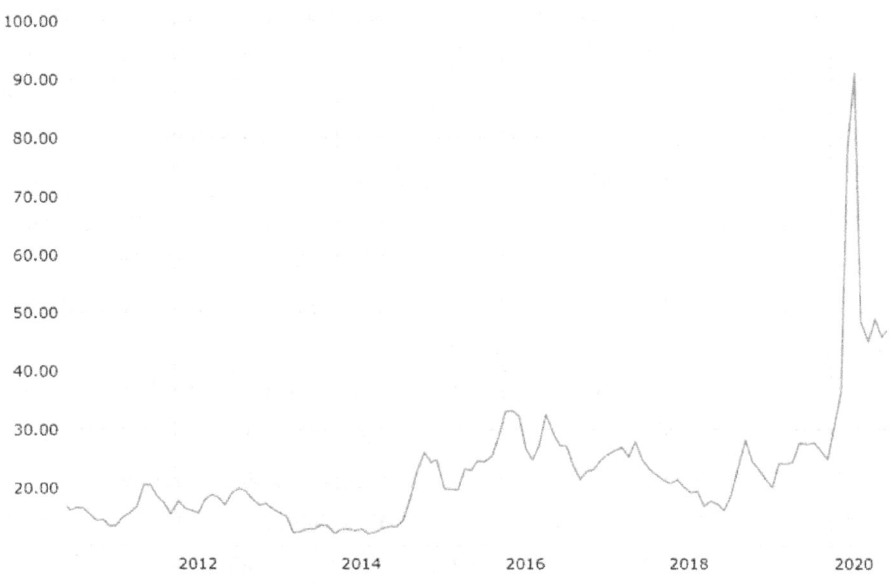

*(Chart: Gold/Oil ratio 2010 to 2020)*

As the chart shows, this relationship has become distended as a result of the crisis. There's now a near 50:1 relationship as of August 2020. This may imply oil is actually quite cheap, gold is expensive, or that the ratio no longer holds. There has been a multitude of media articles heralding the death of oil, and it's certainly true that demand in certain areas has fallen, e.g., airlines and driving to work, but in others, it may rise, e.g., more plastic packaging for food, like supermarkets, another big crisis winner, sell more. There is one big place where it could be said *Oil is the new Oil,* and that is related to data. It seems to have missed the attention of many that all of this data - everyone's Facebook posts, Instagram images, or cloud software solution is stored on a server somewhere that requires electrical power to run. For sure, in the case of one Instagram post, that electrical consumption is miniscule, but multiply it across a world of 7 billion people, and you get an idea now of the immense electrical power required. Oil, natural gas, and coal are still heavily used in electrical power generation across the globe.

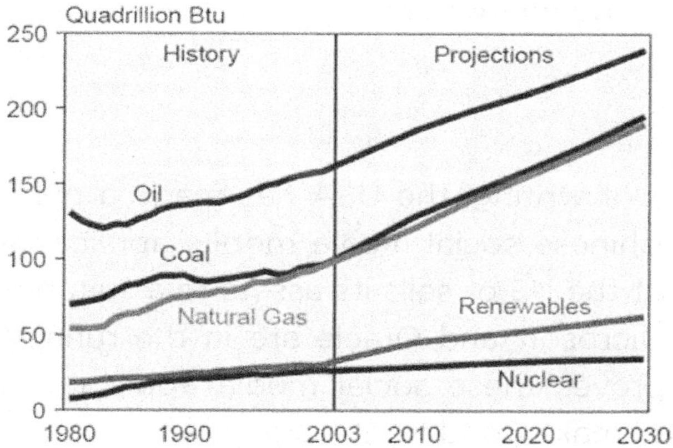


*(Chart: Actual and predicted power sources to 2030)*

The eagle-eyed among you may have spotted the chart dates from 2003. This was deliberate since more recent data shows it to be correct. If so, the future trend for oil consumption is still upward.

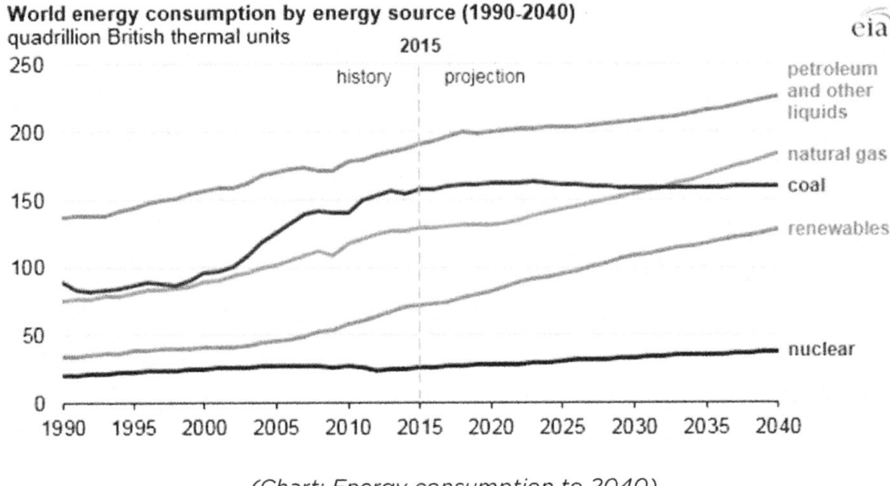


*(Chart: Energy consumption to 2040)*

So, and this is only a question, not investment advice, maybe oil itself is not finished yet as an investment, and its future graph will more closely represent technology and data growth than you might think?

## DATA WARS

At the time of writing, the USA has made a public issue of 'TikTok', a Chinese social media mobile application needing to either exit the US or sells its assets to a suitable US suitor. Currently, Microsoft and Oracle are in the running to make a deal. It proves these social media applications are very valuable and make good front-page news.

National security concerns are being stated. Without being an insider, it's hard to know if the valuable data is the real issue, the location where the data is stored is the issue, or whether TikTok has become so popular a US competitor is using crony capitalism to eliminate the competition. Or even another reason. Whatever the real reasons for this, it proves that gaining screen time and data from people is very, very valuable. It's doubtless one of the future battlefields between power blocs.

# LOSING OUR RELIGION

"Religion is the opium of the people"

— Karl Marx

Religion is the absolute classic example of where following the money can take you, and an absolutely classic example of the informal empires that have operated for thousands of years, quietly transcending national borders, with their own agenda. It's certainly a case study for how corporations *could* become empires as described in **The Road from Democracy to Corporatocracy** - just look at the worldwide spread of the Roman Catholic Empire, for example.

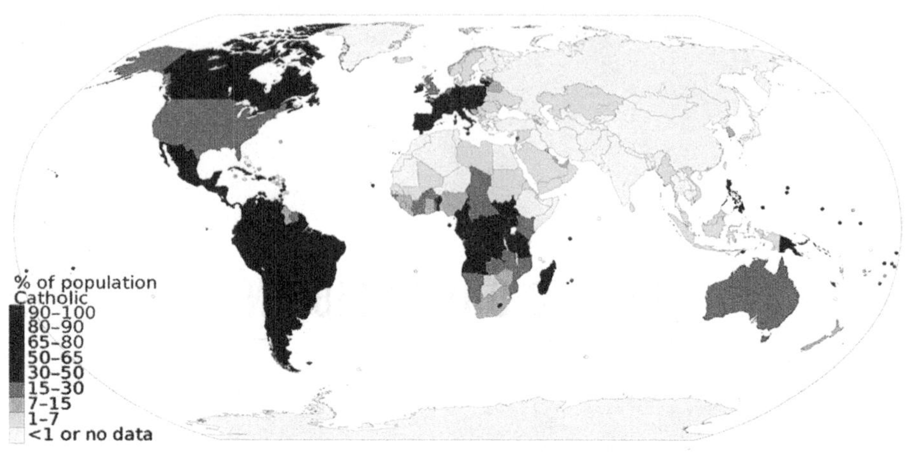


*(Chart: Catholic empire, By Pharexia CC BY-SA 4.0)*

As an imperial power, the Vatican City, an enclave of a few square miles in Rome, Italy, presents immense power and again, those symbols of imperial might - the large buildings, ornate columns, and strong city walls. It only became officially independent of Italy in 1929, but the history goes back much further. We can only guess what's behind those huge walls, stored inside the vaults. The gold, the silver, the ancient texts of immense knowledge. The Vatican does indeed have all the hallmarks of an imperial base, including two leaders - A White Pope and a higher Black Pope. Then, its own central bank, the Vatican Bank, or "Institute for the Works of Religion." If one bank in the world maintains a good reserve ratio against real hard assets, it may well be this one. Even when World War 2 was underway, both sides, Germany and the Allies, respected the neutrality of the Vatican City when occupying Rome and did not enter.

It's worth noting that while the Vatican claims to represent Christianity, other facets of the Christian faith are older, like Coptic Orthodox Christianity. The main representatives of Orthodox are Russia and Greece, but it's a little publicised fact that there are large Christian populations in countries like Ethiopia, Egypt, Lebanon, Palestine, Syria, and Iraq. Some of the early Popes even came from Syria. In Northern Europe, there are large Protestant populations in Germany, Scandinavia, and the United Kingdom, plus the migrants of those countries in the USA, Canada, and Australia.

Then we have Islam, with its power base in Mecca, Saudi Arabia.

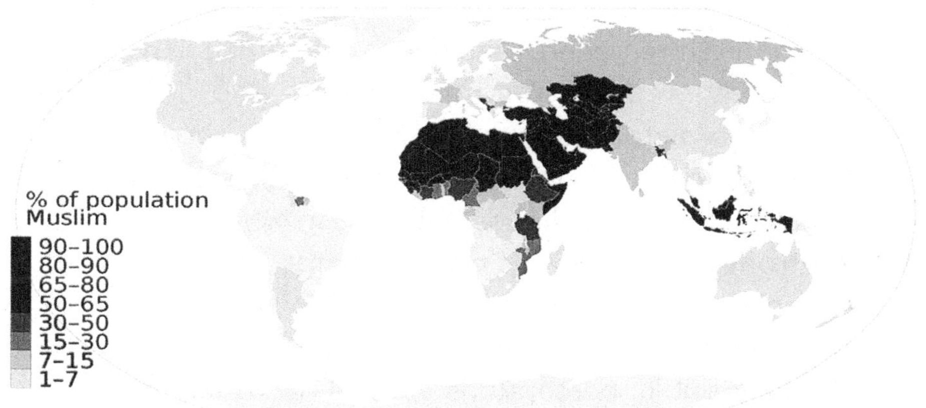


*(Chart of Islamic Empire, source: Wikipedia By M Tracy Hunter - Own work, CC BY-SA 3.0)*

Just like nation-states, religion has been responsible for many wars and continues to be so. From modern terrorist acts, apparently based on religious hatred, to ancient medieval wars like the crusades. Often accompanying these wars, there is a shift of the wealth, the gold and silver to the winning side. During the medieval era in Europe, leading into the reformation of the 1500s and establishment of Protestantism, the church grew immensely rich, angering people living at subsistence level who were expected to contribute despite hardship, seeing their local monks living in luxury while they struggled. This is why there are so many ruined abbeys in places like the UK, these symbols of wealth were often destroyed in anger, and the wealth redistributed. Whether the wealth made its way to the poor people it originally belonged to is another question, but 'freeing up economic resources' is a common theme in Religion throughout history.

Something strange has happened as of 2020, where we may be seeing the end of the Church and religion in its current form. Group worshipping has been banned in many countries, and churches are closed. Traditionally important festivals like Easter, harvest festivals and Christmas didn't happen or are threatened. Significant events like christenings, confirmations, weddings and funerals are also disrupted or cancelled completely. How that will affect the population and their spiritual needs is unclear, but history tells us there have been major religious switches in the past, where the Romans moved from their gods to Christianity, for example. Could it lead to new deities or saints, like a Saint William of Seattle?

We may consider it a joke now but look, for example, at how quickly public perceptions change. It's only a few years since European countries like France and Denmark passed laws banning face coverings in shops and public places. Ostensibly it was called "Ban the Burka" and supposedly directed towards the creep of the more extreme facets of Muslim religion creeping into western society. The reality was uncovered; however, when the first conviction and fine in Denmark was for a white man wearing a motorcycle helmet. Fast forward to the present day, and you're more likely to suffer abuse in a shop for not wearing a face covering. The "Ban the Burka" campaign has been completely forgotten. Would people of a future year believe a story saying the following - that women were 100 times more likely to carry the virus, the virus could exist on human hair, and that black face coverings were more likely to suppress the spread than any other colour? If so - then hey presto! The Burka has been introduced as standard equipment for all women, everywhere.

Whatever people want to wear is probably not a concern for others, and any laws in that way can be regarded as a form of censorship. You could argue that if you intend to travel on a bus, using a discount fare card and the driver asks you to prove your photo id, then you should do that or pay the full fare, but that's probably about it.

In summary, religion has a lot of power and wealth, yet people don't consider it to be a form of empire. It has the power to decide, or at least influence world decisions, and in the recent past, it has been used to justify major wars, mould public opinion, and undoubtedly do so again. It may even be doing it right now, as you read this, and it could be argued that the last two empires - The U.K. and U.S.A. were Protestant Christian, then the two before - France and Spain, where Catholic Christian. Who knows what denomination the next empire will be?

Just think of religion as another area where it pays to follow the money.

# DEFLATION

"Only when the tide goes out, do you discover who's been swimming naked."

— Warren Buffett

Deflation, a general decrease in prices across the whole economy, could also occur at some point. Throughout the whole book, we've talked about an increases in prices as the almost inevitable consequence of fiat currency debasement through the creation of extra currency units, and indeed it is. However, with all the talking of wars, it's worth looking at what happens when a nation is placed on a war footing.

For what is the Corona crisis but a wartime footing? The entire population is being told they are under attack from an enemy; it doesn't really matter if the enemy is a neighbouring country, aliens, or an unseen virus. Being told you're under attack has the same effect - it makes people frightened, less capable of rational thought, and largely paralysed. It also makes you more vulnerable to doing what you are told will help protect you, and it's already showing in terms of people travelling less, spending less, and staying at home more. The campaign to *#StayatHome* has become so successful that there are now concerns that some people may never venture outside ever again. It's certainly one for psychologists and sociologists to ponder, perhaps even researching and writing books about it someday.

Spending less is easy to explain. What do most of us do in a time of crisis and uncertainty? Save and hoard. We're uncertain we'll actually have an income in six months, so we tread carefully when it comes to purchases. So in this respect, the government currency creation right now may not really matter, as most of it will just sit, dormant in people's accounts until the general mood changes. Another reason for this is that items people generally spend money on - a new car, foreign holidays are deemed unnecessary, or there simply aren't the options available right now. Indeed, travelling has turned into something of a risk, with announcements of less than a day's notice meaning thousands of holidaymakers coming back from mainstream holiday destinations like Spain and France were suddenly expected to self-quarantine for 2 weeks on their return to the UK. This is all ultimately going to make people think twice about doing it in the future.

This could lead to deflation, as less and less money actually circulates in the economy, with more and more of it squirrelled away or used to repay existing debt. If no-one is taking out loans, then there could also be less new money entering the economy.

A precedent for this has been set in wartime. It's the same in terms of uncertainty and rationing, meaning people spend no more than necessary. As discussed previously, Weimar republic Germany in 1921-23 suffered huge inflation, but what's not really mentioned is that inflation of the currency also took place dramatically back during the war, 1914-18 period, without any major increase in prices. The reason being that there was little to spend money on, so the extra currency paid out, for example, to soldiers simply made its way into banks, drawers, and tins, ready for a rainy day. The problem was, for those who returned from the war, the rainy day happened all at once, and a tidal wave of money began to hit, pushing prices up dramatically in a very short time in 1919-20, before the 1921-23 tidal wave.

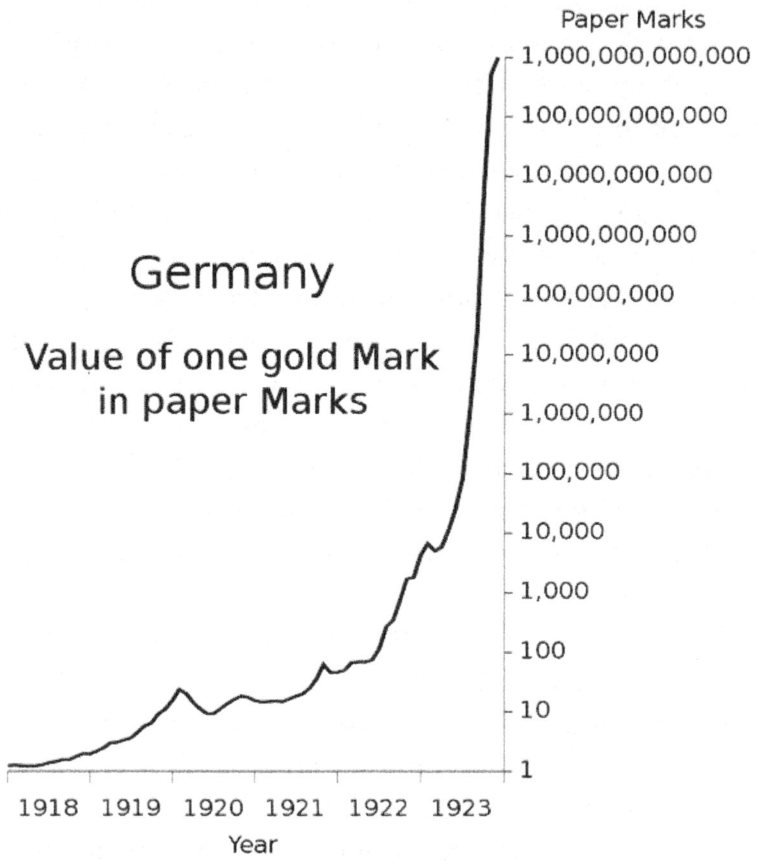


*(Chart: German WW1 Inflation, source: Wikipedia By Delphi234 - Own work, CC0)*

A similar thing also occurred in 1929-32, after the Wall Street Crash of 1929. It's little reported that the stock market didn't actually hit its final nadir until 1932 - some 90% below the 1929 peak. During this time, prices fell dramatically, and unemployment was huge - all economic uncertainty factors that affect many people - they simply won't part with what money they have got. Who can blame them?

*(Chart: DJIA 1929-32. Source: Wikipedia by Encik Tekateki - Own work, CC BY-SA 4.0)*

Maybe we can expect a similar thing to happen again?

There are several big issues with this, being right that it may occur, the timing of when it will occur, and how long it will last. Government power to go on a Keynesian-style spending spree is much bigger than in 1918 or 1929, to prevent deflation, which they hate as it destroys their whole tax base and ability to borrow more money. The sad thing is, of course, that for most people, deflation is the greatest thing going, as it means the things they need to buy normally get cheaper. Deflation was a built-in feature of the Gold Standard that existed before 1914 - prices very rarely rose unless there was a genuine shortage of something and were wont to fall if technological improvements in manufacturing and agriculture meant something could be produced cheaper.

You've probably worked out by now that deflation can also be deliberately manufactured and that some entities can profit a lot from a period of deflation, obtaining assets on the cheap as homeowners default on their mortgages and businesses are unable to repay loans or pay tax bills when trade dries up. This is especially true of a fiat currency, where control and issuance are centralised. To decide whether deflation will occur, it would be wise to look for clues. Some that look to be true of the Corona crisis include:-

- A period where household incomes and business incomes decline dramatically

- A period where it becomes harder to borrow new money. These newly-created loans are what helps inflation by increasing currency units already in existence. In the U.K., for example, banks increased the deposit limits for new homebuyers, so that in many cases, a 25% deposit is now required to buy a house.

- A period of extreme uncertainty, where households and businesses cut back on non-essential spending. Like wartime. In this situation, the focus may be on repaying the existing debts. Instead of taking out new ones on consumer debit and credit cards, for example.

- A period of inflation in key commodities, meaning less free income for 'luxury extras' - food is showing some rises already.

- A period where governments may increase the tax burden to cover extra debt payments incurred by the crisis.

Assuming deflation were to occur, you would still want to hold gold and silver, as well as fiat currency units. You probably wouldn't want to be holding too many of the assets that would be exposed to a deflationary environment, where the tidal wave of fiat currency floating around dries up - property and stocks, for example. In the case of property, prices could fall dramatically, and loans are much harder to repay. Again cheaper property is good news for the many, who have been priced out of the market for many years now and rent from the other side of the equation - landlords with an empire of properties built on an empire of debt. The real question is - for how long would your government allow deflation to happen, even if it does happen?

For those wishing to "follow the money," Legendary investor Warren Buffett has record high cash levels in his investment company, Berkshire Hathaway. He often laments that there are simply '…No deals worth doing…', then in 2020, he also made an interesting move, Berkshire announced a stake in one of the world's biggest gold miners, Barrick Gold. Maybe there will indeed be a period when the government just can't or won't prevent deflation, and it will prove wise to make sure you keep your trunks on at all times but watch for those who didn't. Buffett is another case where it can pay to follow the money.

# PART 3

# INTO THE FUTURE

"It's the End of the World as we know it, and I feel fine."

— REM

Having talked about the major changes that may be coming and their effects on society, the planet, and most importantly - our wealth, let's admit it, a lot of it sounds bad. The major change is that we are entering a major new era.

## THE TECHNOLOGICAL ERA

Now for some good news - just as people prospered in the agricultural era and industrial era, people will survive and prosper in the technological era.

Probably. Technology can and should be a massive force for the good of humanity. For example, this book wouldn't exist without it. It got written on word-processing software, and it's published using print-on-demand, from an electronic copy. What you hold in your hand now or regard with your eyes exemplifies that good things are indeed possible with technology and the internet. You probably bought it using online means, too, with online digital payment. The problems today with technology seem to be around ethics and freedom.

In a way, it's not too dissimilar to the beginning of the industrial era. People who had been used to the outdoors and clean air on farms now had to put up with fumes, pollution, and squalid conditions in the cities, struggling to cope with the number of new entrants. The pollution and awful death statistics, especially amongst young children and the massive upheavals of families from the countryside to cities and emigration, was the price paid. For the technological era, the price paid may come in other ways. Here are some suggestions:-

1. Pollution - The new pollution may well be high radiation levels from devices like Mobile phones, Wifi, 5G, and smart meters. The WHO has had this type of radiation on their list since 2012 as a possible carcinogen. Unlike the smokestacks and polluted rivers, this pollution is undetectable by sight or smell.

2. Job Losses - Many job sectors that seemed safe even a year ago have been annihilated. Transport, restaurants, hotels, and holidays, for example. Many of these jobs may never come back. Just like those agricultural tillers.

3. Overcrowding - Many families had to get used to a crowded house, with everyone home. The children are off school or studying from home, and both parents are expected to work from home if they were still lucky enough to have a job. This has already led to families often needing to develop rotas, so everyone's needs were attended to

4. Physical Health - Sitting in front of screens will bring a whole load of new ailments. In fact, it already is.

Repetitive strain injury (RSI) was first identified in the 90s from keyboard overuse. Eye strain from LED screens, even from school projectors, may be responsible for more children needing glasses. Then there's obesity, already an issue in recent years, but if your work and leisure are both spent in front of screens inside your home, how much exercise might some of us get? Just like Rickets from a poor diet 200 years ago, or a lack of vitamin D from not getting enough sunlight. Either because of long hours inside a factory or a life under permanent smoke-filled skies.

5. Mental Health - Whereas the big diseases of the industrial revolution were things like cholera, mental health due to stress through lost work, being forced to stay at home, or a huge reduction in social contact could become a bigger factor in the future.

The Technological era has already resulted in an unexpected return to something largely eliminated during the Industrial era - working from home. 200+ years ago, many things that were not industrialised were traditionally done by individuals in their own homes. Textiles, metalwork, and even the making of beer are examples of this. If this trend continues or becomes permanent, then traditional town and city centre facilities catering to commuters may struggle. There are already signs of this occurring - hotels, shops, and restaurants catering to the needs of office workers are closing or being repurposed, so they are not exposed to lost markets.

## THE GREAT RESET

You may recall the World Economic forum referring to 2020 as "The Great Reset" and how it conjures up images of an ailing PC or smartphone, needing to be switched off and on, with a major clearout of the memory, the freeing up of space and deletion of unwanted apps. Most of us would agree with that. However, it seems that the reset, in this case, has retained many of the Apps that should be deleted. For example:-

Government version 9.11 - The big government surveillance society that has accelerated around the millennium, the one that curtails individual rights and freedoms, culminating in introducing a variety of regulations in 2020 to restrict your travel and ability to transact and trade with fellow human beings to survive. In any other era, that would be called fascism. In 2017, the then U.K. Prime Minister Theresa May referred to a terrorist attack as "hating us for our freedoms." The irony of that should not be lost on any of us, for just three years later, we have no freedoms now too. Even your right to self-expression is gone, as you now have to wear a mask that hides the facial expressions that go with what you say. When wearing a mask, it's probably not a good time to make ironic or sarcastic jokes with a hidden smile.

Fiat currency version x.x (many regional variations of this app exist) - be it pounds, euros, dollars, yen or pesos, fiat currency still exists, and if anything, the great reset means even more increasing amounts of it in circulation, devaluing any savings you might have. Fortunately, there are now apps you can install that operate outside or complement Fiat Currency version x. However, this app is incredibly hard to remove and remains essential for most right now.

Medical care 2020 - Once upon a time, there were these two words, 'health' and 'care.' The meaning of the two words is obvious, and someone put them together to form one word "healthcare" - the act of looking after your health. In reality, this word means doing things such as eating a varied diet of good foods. Hence, you get all of the vitamins and minerals required. Then, taking exercise such as long walks, and avoiding doing damaging things like smoking - which, ironically, doctors in the 1950s even claimed could cure asthma. Modern medical care is extremely removed from this, and a trip to the doctors' surgery or hospital has become more akin to visiting a Moroccan bazaar when the meeting is seen as a sales opportunity to thrust all kinds of items with a commission for the seller your way. How about a blood pressure test? It's high, oh, these drugs might help - completely ignoring that it's high because of the bad traffic or long wait you had getting to the Doctor's surgery. On birth control already? No problem, how about trying this new product instead? Want to go home and be independent after a hospitalisation? No problem Mr/Mrs Jones; we just need to sort out the right care package for you; just sign here. Often, people get stuck on a direct debit of medical care to take for life, rather than dealing with the core premise of their *health care*. This app is growing so big; it's taking up all the resources on your smartphone. In the future, it may even store your COVID-19 test pass certificate, too, along with Microsoft's proposed ID 2020 inoculation history - if there's space. You may have to show them to be able to even travel, attend a football match or concert, should those things ever open up again.

Education 4.18 - This app will get you used to the prison mentality and prepare you for your future role as a low-level member of the proletariat in society. Unfortunately, the free version of this app will give you no financial education whatsoever, so that you remain blissfully unaware of what money is and how it works. This is partly because you're planned to be a consumer of financial products that you don't understand, to help fund your own future slavery, as described in **50 percent a Slave**. There are paid-for versions of this App in most countries that provide a much higher quality experience and will prepare you better for a role in the upper echelons of society, with a high up role in Government 9.11 a possibility. The paid-for versions are extremely expensive. However, the advanced app Education 18.23 has no free option, and everyone must pay for it - over a large number of years, through something called a student loan, issued in fiat currency, and requiring repayment with interest added. Already in life, we find the creation of money as loans, to be repaid with interest added, as the biggest financial manipulation going and the best means of chaining down the slaves early.

Work 18.65 - After the reboot, many people found that this app had actually been removed from their phones. Despite the fact, most of them still wanted or needed to use it. Many others found the terms and conditions had changed dramatically, and there was no way to reverse that if you wanted to continue to use the app. Work 18.65 might soon see a massive series of swift upgrades - Work 18.99 is even a strong possibility in the not-too-distant future. Others, meanwhile, are finding it difficult ever to download the app again.

Bluetooth - this innocuous little button that you may sometimes use to wirelessly broadcast music to a local device or your car has now taken on a new sinister aspect after the upgrade. Other smartphones in the vicinity, in the pockets of other users, now have apps harvesting your Device ID, the unique ID that can be used to track down your telephone, and ultimately, you. Did you consent to this? Some technology experts even claim that with Bluetooth turned off, your telephone is still detectable by other smartphones.

If our lives are increasingly digital, then the smartphone Apps analogy isn't a bad one to think about. Whether our lives should be increasingly digital, or we are signing away, some of our humanity is beyond the bounds of this book. However, moving back to money - remember that real money is physical: gold and silver - the fake money now is digital, so don't confuse real and fake for the same thing in any aspect of our lives, may well be the best way to look at it. It's also a good time to plant a seed in our minds of the Apps we would like to see if smartphones and the internet are going to work *with and for* humanity, not against it.

We've ended up in a situation where the internet is used for everything in life - finance, shopping, work, and entertainment. While this has given us freedom in some ways, the reliance has become so pronounced that it leaves us vulnerable to censorship and restrictions on choices. Even if no-one did deliberately censor the internet - a theoretical argument anyway, since YouTube is constantly deleting content and entire channels, as is Facebook, then there's always a chance that the *Machine stops*. The network on which the internet itself is built could one day just simply break down, either for hours, days, or permanently if the skills no longer existed to maintain it. What would you do? How would you survive? This concept was actually explored in a book by E.M. Forster in 1909, "The Machine Stops." In it, he predicted a futuristic world where people live in small single cells and are hooked into what a machine tells them, so they get all of their knowledge and information from the machine. As the book progresses, the machine begins to break down, and there are no longer people around with the knowledge to fix it. Considering E.M. Forster's main literature legacy is "Brideshead Revisited," it was a most unusual story for him to write.

The future is going to bring many new developments, changes, and challenges. Since the internet developed, it's been largely seen as a good thing, yet in recent years we have begun to see a decline in the freedom, choice, and human side of the technology. In a way, it's a magnified version of what happened in the 1980s, when young people built computer games by themselves, or the 1990s and 2000s, when people built their own websites and blogs. Then the big corporations moved in, and all of the internet traffic redirected to just a few main sites. Facebook has also helped massively in this:-

| Site | Type | Principal country/territory |
|---|---|---|
| Google Search | Internet services and products | United States |
| YouTube | Video sharing | United States |
| Baidu | Internet-related services and products | China |
| Tencent QQ | Portal | China |
| Sohu | Portal | China |
| Facebook | Social networking | United States |
| Taobao | Online shopping | China |
| Haosou | Internet security and web search engine | China |
| Jingdong Mall | E-commerce | China |
| Yahoo! | Portal and media | United States |
| Amazon | E-commerce and cloud computing | United States |
| Wikipedia | Encyclopedia | United States |
| Sina Corp | Portal and instant messaging | China |
| Sina Weibo | Social networking | China |
| Windows Live | Software plus services | United States |
| Zoom Video Communications | Videotelephony | United States |
| Reddit | Social news and entertainment | United States |
| Netflix | Streaming TV and movies | United States |
| Xinhua News Agency | News | China |
| Okezone | Portal | Indonesia |

*(Chart: top 20 internet websites visited, August 2020. Source: Alexa/Wikipedia)*

## WHAT NEXT

What happens next is only conjecture, but Hollywood gives us plenty of clues, with more dystopian films such as Bladerunner and Game of Thrones. To summarise:-

Humans have been separated from the ability to transact with each other directly, without anyone else involved. Be it through regulations, taxes, or monitoring, next to no transactions these days are conducted without outside influence.

Humans have been gradually separated from true money, gold and silver. We now transact in a single notional currency backed by nothing but trust and enforced by law. These currencies are now in their final death throes in relation to their original gold value. Remember how One Pound Sterling is now worth 0.004% of its original value? We are living through the era of the final 1% of government fiat currencies.

Human freedom has been massively eroded, and the majority has not noticed. David Icke refers to this as the *Totalitarian Tiptoe*, in his thought-provoking book "Phantom Self." Had these measures been implemented in one go, people would've resisted and fought back, but by doing things gradually, over a large number of years, we have ended up where we are today as a society. Forgetting what real money is, following rules set by a third party, and continually still believing this higher entity is setting those rules for us for our own good.

As of 2020, humans are now being separated from each other.

After 200 to 300 years, nation-states are in decline. Taxation methods are maxed-out, with many of us now **50 percent a slave**, if not more.

Democracy as a system is on the wane. It's debatable whether it ever really existed, but the illusion has become harder to maintain. The UK being a recent prime example of it happening more prominently in a supposed first-world 'free' nation, where the wishes of the majority to leave the European Union have been ignored and gradually watered down to near-nothingness.

Corporations, a relatively new invention in the history of mankind, are more powerful, globalised, and rich then they ever have been.

## NATION STATES

The only solution to gaining more wealth for many nation-states seems to be to invade and exploit other territories not already harvested, and/or begin turning inwards on the stored wealth of their own citizens.

So, who are the fattest meat cows in most countries for the nation-state to go after? Two immediate ones spring to mind, the old and the middle class. The old are already a prime target; just think about how the Corona crisis has begun to separate them from the rest of society, in ways which no-one would've accepted just a year ago. Now, Granny must only be viewed in the old people's home behind a police tape-style cordon, waved at from a distance, perhaps occasionally viewed on a tablet through a skype call - if a nurse can be found to help her master the technology, that is. If Granny or Grandpa is unlucky enough to get ill, well, the hospital may help manoeuvre you towards the 'right' decision of letting them die. So much for the Hippocratic Oath. The main difference with **The Crown** era is that now they must be stuck in a room as the clock ticks down, alone, their relatives remote, no chance of a last family goodbye. The old have other immediate advantages for harvesting compared to the middle class - they are less able to fight back physically, they tend to absorb more mainstream media, trusting what is presented to them, and have a historical relationship with Nanny that goes further back to a period when Nanny was more benevolent and helpful than she is now. That the old tend to have more wealth than the young is likely a natural consequence of being alive more years and having lived through a time when it was easier to save and accumulate wealth - taxes and state interference were not so intense then as they are now. The old also tend to be more active consumers of medical care products and less active economically, which means fewer commissions in terms of income for the nation-state and corporations. All factors that count against them. Think of inheritance tax as the government commission on every death they can engineer. Poor old people, even with Brexit, they were demonised as robbing the future of the young. Yet, in the UK, many voted to leave the European Union because they have memories of full employment, better, freer times, and wanted them back for future generations.

The middle class are not safe, probably merely next on the list. The annoying thing about them is that in addition to having accumulated wealth, they tend to have opinions too and are not afraid to express them because they have savings to protect. For now, anyway. Karl Marx didn't like the middle class for these very reasons.

Corporations and big business generally were once a big nation-state target for increased revenue. This simply isn't the case anymore, in most jurisdictions. Corporations, especially the multi-nationals, have become adept at shifting costs and profits to where they are treated best. This means that governments will turn to those with fewer avoidance options. Citizens and their small businesses. The new legislation, like the updated IR35 in the UK, suggests this is happening already. Another possibility mooted is a new property tax on land value.

The revenue collection could also extend outside borders, as struggling nations look to militarily or diplomatically acquire the resources of neighbouring countries, which may be prospering relatively, or have less debt and larger gold reserves. It's already happened, with the resource-rich nations of Afghanistan, Iraq, and Libya, but not so successful in Syria, yet. The enjoyable film "Three Kings," starring an actor talked about as a possible future president, George Clooney, even softened us up to the US military liberating and redistributing middle-eastern gold reserves as part of their 1991 mission. This is no different from the reasons for many wars hundreds and thousands of years ago. The winning side plunders and pillages the loot. With the Middle East already experiencing that, when you look at the world map Russia and Africa could have much to offer. Although Russia has strong military defence capabilities and China has informally colonised much of Africa - it's already estimated over a million Chinese are living there, cutting deals, mining, and building infrastructure. John Perkins' book 'Confessions of an Economic Hitman' is superb in revealing the diplomatic and financial ways that the USA gained control of much of South America, without too many shots being fired. Great Britain also did a similar thing in India, enabling them to control a country much larger in size and population.

Nation-states may even fragment into smaller and smaller units, as people turn on distant capitals that they feel no longer represent or look after them. The referendums in Scotland to gain independence from the UK and in Catalonia, Spain, suggest this is a growing trend. Barbarians in 410 AD sacked Rome itself, but it's open to conjecture whether any of the 'barbarians' were, in fact, angry ex-citizens of the empire. Note, though, that while they fragment, they may continue to survive on the world map but as puppets of other, larger entities. Conversely, the capitals themselves may decide, if they are still generating wealth, to secede from the nation-state itself. Especially true of city ports whose economic and ethnic makeup is increasingly becoming detached from the rest of the nation-state it purports to represent. London, Dublin, and Copenhagen are possible future European examples of this. Vancouver and the Western Coast US Tech cities possible North American examples that may secede and attempt to avoid a future Romanesque Barbarian sacking.

The Nanny states people got used to are in decline. As already discussed, Nanny has become a dark shadowy omnipresent, austere Victorian nanny, rather than the happy and light 1960s "Mary Poppins", popularised in the film of the same name. There is some irony that one of the campaigns in the UK, during **The Crown**, that won people over was #SaveTheNHS - at the exact time that the NHS stopped providing many of the services that save lives and shipped old people out to care homes, in many cases increasing the Corona death statistics. With the likely future rise of UBI, digital currency, and data collection, it feels like at some point it will even stop being a universal healthcare system and make assessments of whether people are worthy of help, with deductions for, say, non-vaccinations, smoking, drinking alcohol or being overweight. Again the powers that be seem to be preparing us for this with the COVID-19 Health passport for Premier League footballers, Boris Johnson's alleged weight-loss announcement, and carefully placed stories on 'binge drinking.' Linking the last two to increased costs on the NHS. In Argentina, you already cannot even get a driving licence or passport without proof of vaccinations, and other nations will probably try to introduce similar laws.

## HUMAN BEINGS

Now you've heard about Nanny and how she's not really that interested in looking after you anymore, it doesn't necessarily mean she won't still *pretend* to care. One of the likeliest trends is that the furlough scheme mentioned in **The Crown** becomes a Universal Basic Income, or UBI. It's not hard to imagine that UBI begins with publicity as a supposedly benevolent thing, but once in place, it begins to take on a more Orwellian face, with deductions for unacceptable behaviour. At first, it would be fines where other citizens would believe "serves them right," as with benefit sanctions in the UK, but the totalitarian goose-step could creep to lesser crimes like the Facebook post or tweet you just did. Your dissent would soon disappear, knowing you'd get fewer UBI credits in your account, wouldn't it?

In the future, when you have millions of people dependent on receiving money from the state, based on certain criteria, then all you need to do is tweak the criteria and adjust the money taps to each citizen individually. This would never have been possible once, but with the rise of technology, many things now are, and more will be in the future.

Let's look at other factors which may come to affect us. For example:-

- Your healthcare may suffer dramatically. The crisis has caused, is causing, and will cause more physical and psychological problems with stress. Then getting used to the corporate push towards changing work practices, like home-working. Not just home-working, but education timetables for 2020 are beginning to make clear that children are no longer expected to come to school much, but attend classes at home, via a PC. It's interesting that in recent years, governments and corporations were both onto this already with campaigns such as 'It's OK not to be OK,' encouraging people to talk openly about their personal lives and traumas.

- That crime can rise dramatically when there are upheavals, and large scale disruptions of income and food are given throughout history. Morals and fairness can disappear quickly in a crisis.

- Less babies may be born the next few years due to the restrictions on meeting up, staying in the house, and the uncertainty around future income prospects, even for established couples. This is yet to be seen but could cause a massive ripple some years in the future when a dearth of young people enter the education system and later, the job market - especially if their taxes are still expected to keep the government Ponzi scheme going. That pornography sites now appear in the top 50 most-visited worldwide websites may be another sign real relationships are dying.

- An attempt to split the generations. The demonisation and alienation of old people is entering a new phase. If public perception of this can be stretched a bit further, enforced euthanasia is also a future possibility at some point. On the other side, parents temporarily enjoyed more time with children during the 'lockdown' part of the Corona crisis. However, the trend since the 1900s has been ever more the other way, with children institutionalised from an earlier-and-earlier age and schools beginning to look more like penitentiaries than part of the community.

- Racially, the make-up of the world is also changing. As a proportion of the population, whites are massively in decline, and given who the countries of the current empire are, any upheavals in their prospects will only make the decline more pronounced. It's estimated that only 10% of the world population is white, compared to around 33% in 1900. This is another relevant factor in considering which religions will rise and which will fall

While working from home has become a major early trend of the 'Great Reset,' this contradicts one of the likely long-term outcomes of the Technological era. Even greater urbanisation than ever before. During the Industrial Revolution, people migrated to the cities for work, but later on, they also migrated to areas with services for modern life, like transport links, gas, electricity, and piped water. The reasons for this future migration may be similar; to be in reach of the technology infrastructure, people are relying on more and more and deemed just as essential to life. As office workers, retailers, and sandwich sellers migrate or close; the buildings may be turned into high-density accommodation for the smart cities of the future.

Country living may decline further because people have also become distanced from the land that once supplied their needs. Fewer than ever know how to grow their own vegetables. As seen by the fight for the toilet rolls at supermarkets, instead of fights for fruit and vegetables, or in the seed aisle of your local DIY shop. Some USA states, like Michigan, even outlawed the sale of seeds during the crisis. It can already be seen that financially it's becoming harder to survive in the modern era if you live remotely from others. Rural public transport is dying, fewer and fewer people are self-sufficient, and you are remote from supermarkets or even a decent broadband connection. Taxation is also becoming slanted towards encouraging people to live in smaller spaces. Denmark, for example, is increasing property taxes on the amount of ground you own, which clearly means those in apartments are unaffected, compared to those with a suburban house with even a reasonable-sized garden. All this is already having an urbanisation effect, but it will only get worse. There is great investment going on right now in smart city infrastructure. It fits that the technology era would prefer more and more people living in closer proximity because data collection is harder when people are spread out rurally. Get people into the same space, and the data-gathering possibilities are immense. Airports have known this for many years, with surveys even gathering Bluetooth data from telephones to assess footfall, traffic spots, and average time spent in airports. All valuable data for retailers and rental prices. It probably already goes on elsewhere too, with us unaware.

Again, Hollywood has prepared us for this with many futuristic films. A few to consider would be - 'Total Recall,' 'Bladerunner' and 'Game of Thrones', but there are many, many more. People always live in sanitised modern buildings, sleeping in small single room cells with a big screen. A clean, minimalist, modern lifestyle. Very few futuristic films even present any concept of nature still existing and those that do, like 'Bladerunner II,' present a destroyed, vegetation-free scorched earth, with plants grown in greenhouses. Next time you watch any such film, just ponder for a moment on the data-gathering that is implied as the stars talk to their TV set or are chased by police, who can track their every move via various devices.

Democracy is dying. Just before the crisis began, there were huge protests in Hong Kong, Paris, and South America, among others. Now governments worldwide have introduced restrictions on gatherings, giving the reason to lessen the spread of Covid-19. It has the effect of preventing any visible dissent happening again in the future. On Brexit specifically, **The Crown** may be the final nail in the coffin for this. After months of near-silence, the government and media may announce late in 2020 that the crisis is too great to fight alone, so the UK will rejoin, or remain in the current situation of no say but still sending tribute. There may even be a new referendum to 'prove' this change of heart. Again, there can be no Brexit robbery protests - in the UK, the Corona law restricts gatherings of more than six people. The EU also has a history of second referenda if the first result doesn't go a certain way - just ask Ireland and Denmark. The Corona casualties - many of them old people, may also be used as an excuse for any change in the referendum result. Killing multiple birds with one stone by achieving the Brexit outcome desired and driving a wedge further between the generations for the future wealth collection purposes already mentioned.

The world generally is increasingly suffering from a new ailment - *Selective Democracy Disorder*, or SDD. Again, events in 2020 really highlighted this. Some people attempted to form protest groups against their loss of livelihoods and freedom using social media. There are plenty of stories from the USA, Canada, Australia, and the UK reported by some disbelieving mainstream media commentators about police visiting homes and making arrests of people based on their social media posts. At the same time, it did not miss the attention of even channels like Sky in Australia, that Black Lives Matter (BLM) protests, sometimes also organised via Facebook, went ahead uninhibited with no arrests, full freedom of speech, and a blaze of publicity. Compare the light policing of recent BLM events in the UK, even where there were violent incidents, with the police wearing yellow vests and no protection, versus the police in full body armour, riot shields, and weaponry, facing down French, Chilean, or British Brexit protest marches in 2019. It's clear that some causes are more equal than others. A huge protest against Corona restrictions in Berlin was mentioned in passing by the BBC as being '..A few conspiracy theorists and COVID-19 deniers..', whereas Berlin police said as many as one million people attended. In the long term, some views will be 'right,' and others will be 'wrong,' and you may have to be more careful about voicing the 'wrong' ones you have, in public or close to a smart device.

**The Crown** has also brought about a blurring between laws, regulations, and rules. It's fascinating how this is occurring, with very few people even noticing. For something to become law, it must be debated in parliaments and go through legal steps before being confirmed. Instead, if you listen to your media, you will hear things said in headlines like "New regulations come into force," and then they will proceed with the story as if it was a legal threat to comply. These are not laws. The television media has been terrible, but to their credit, The Daily Telegraph in the UK did actually write articles questioning this new method of parliament 'ruling by decree', as they called it and trying to bypass the whole legal framework of a functioning democracy. To put this in perspective, it's the difference between saying 'Keep off the Grass' and 'Please can you keep off the grass?'. In the second case, there are few to no penalties for not following it. They can try, though, and the worry here is new legal precedents will be set at some point soon to make this the new method of lawmaking. Interestingly, the subtle media language has already referred to politicians more and more in recent years as 'lawmakers' rather than MPs or representatives. This isn't even a UK issue; it's worldwide. Denmark also introduced a quarantine rule for people returning from countries on a specific list - note the word, *rule* - and then had to admit that it had no legal basis and was just a request. If people follow these new rules and regulations as if there were laws, then the whole concept of democracy and freedom will be massively eroded in record time.

Religion remains a powerful controlling force in the background, possibly the best representation of how an empire can last and maintain its wealth, with Christianity now 2,000 years old and Islam over 1,000 years old. It will remain so in the future, for certain religions anyway. Maybe not so for others, as their devotees die off or are killed by the major changes that may be about to happen. New or modified religions may also develop. Religious wars occur even now that we know nothing about or do not even recognise as religious wars. The persecution of the large Christian minorities in Egypt, Syria, and Iraq being a good example. Major religious figures like Jesus and Mohammad seem to have had an aversion to moneylending, and it's worth wondering whether part of their rise was due to representing oppressed peoples in times of hardship. If so, perhaps in a new crisis, a new religion will rise once more.

Royal Families are also great representations of empires that have existed for thousands of years. While ostensibly linked with nation-states as the nation-state rose, their history goes back much, much further. It is one of intermarriage between families, cementing links and transferring vast amounts of wealth between each other, even entire territories containing thousands of people. In 1914, the Kings of three of the major belligerents - George V of England, Tsar Nicholas of Russia, and Kaiser Wilhem of Germany, were in fact, all cousins. To the modern eye, they are presented as safe, reassuring images that bring vast wealth in tourism riches to us all. Step back for a moment and look at the number of assets like valuable real estate they own, along with special privileges such as no income tax for Queen Elizabeth II in the U.K. They are not immune to the future either, as nation-states decline. Indeed, they have thousands of years of history where, as some lines decline other lineages rise and acquire more wealth and power. It is no coincidence that the extreme fiat money inflation in 1790s France coincided with the increased usage of Mademoiselle Guillotine on the French aristocracy. Certainly, just as **The Crown** virus brings big changes for us, it and the aftermath may bring changes for their crowns. Good and bad.

The French revolution highlights another divisive influence that may already be making a comeback, class. Many of us are no longer considered to be working class, having attained higher education, decent jobs, and homeownership - things that our ancestors could never have achieved. However, in the future, social currency of the bad kind could result in a huge underclass, barely subsisting, and unable to access any services or wealth. Then at the other extreme, a new aristocracy, with all the wealth, the best social credit ratings, and the ability to do whatever they like. Who will be amongst this aristocracy is anyone's guess, but fair to assume it will include many in the upper echelons now - royals, landed gentry, rich corporate owners, and politically intermarried families like the Kinnocks in the UK - where Stephen, British MP, is married to Helle Thorning-Schmidt, ex-Danish PM. Yes, class never really went away; it just went underground and may openly reemerge in the future. Campaigns like anti -isms, e.g., sexism, and racism, could be interpreted as attempts to get the proletariat fighting amongst each other again instead of looking up at the real problems, those above now in control of their money and restricting their freedom. Aldous Huxley's 1930s "Brave New World," another view of a futuristic dystopian society, refers to 80% of the population being a member of a group called the proles from birth, and only ever able to attain menial jobs.

We are being encouraged to hate each other, or at least be suspicious, as proven by the success of the snitch hotlines. Remember Goering's comment about denouncing the pacifists in wartime? It's the time honoured tradition of any power to denounce those who don't follow or believe in the official doctrine. For now, it's those not wearing masks, because as you are repeatedly told, masks are not for you, but for other people, right? Almost for certain, the next, perhaps a year or two from now may be those unwilling to submit to whatever vaccine is offered - conveniently forgetting that even the World Health Organisation has the right to refuse vaccines enshrined in choice. Or it did. As we are repeatedly told, it's a wartime situation, and if you're not doing the same as everyone else, then you carry some of the blame. It's not impossible to imagine people being refused access to shops, trains, and the like in the not-too-distant future, with their fellow citizens cheering their discomfort on, exactly like those Jews suffered on the train platforms of Austria back in 1938. After that, who next? The old people? Or, the overweight, smokers and alcoholics, perhaps. Why should they get 'scarce' NHS resources for their self-inflicted issues?

"First, they came for the Socialists,
and I did not speak out—
Because I was not a Socialist.
Then they came for the Trade Unionists,
and I did not speak out—
Because I was not a Trade Unionist.
Then they came for the Jews,
and I did not speak out—
Because I was not a Jew.
Then they came for me—and there
was no one left to speak for me."

— Martin Niemoller

Bearing this World War 2 quote in mind, is it coincidental that it just got a lot easier to incarcerate the uncooperative and the outliers without trial indefinitely? Under the new UK Coronavirus bill of 2020, you will just need one Doctor and a nurse.

## CORPORATIONS

Corporations are on the rise in terms of power and wealth. Many corporations are now more valuable than many nation-states and also have more 'citizens' as employees than many nation-states. Some have become adept at using the machinery of government to tilt the table their way to ensure even more wealth rolls in their direction, through tax avoidance and laws designed to hold back smaller competitors. They have also taken over many of the services that were originally provided by the government. In conjunction with this, welfare state services for all are declining, and it may become more and more of a world where it is 'every man for himself.'

Further, people may migrate in large numbers, fleeing physical and financial persecution from some ailing nations. This migration could also be speeded up by the new work from home that allows people to retain their employment but be based where they wish, which could be viewed as a broadside by the corporations on the weakening nation-states to reduce nation's ability to tax key employees, much the same as some are already adept at avoiding corporation taxes.

Ailing nation-states may choose to align themselves with major corporations, either informally or more formally in the future. Especially if they are smaller but can offer something like access to certain markets, low tax rates, an educated workforce, or have geographical benefits. A classic example of this is Ireland, a sleepy backwater of Europe until the 1990s, but now a member of the European Union. It has become a base for massive corporations such as Google, Microsoft, Dell, Apple, and Amazon. You may have even noticed historic media coverage of claims of tax avoidance and unfair competition on tax rates regarding Ireland and these locations. What you may not have realised is the international reach, way beyond the obvious physical trade. For example, when you connect to a website that runs on Amazon servers in the cloud, it is often in Ireland, even when accessed from faraway locations like India. Another example is Luxembourg, with a massive banking and financial sector out of proportion to its tiny size, but geographically again within the EU and close to the official EU capital, Brussels, where a lot of money and power is right now.

Taken to the logical extreme, corporations, especially the ones bigger than sizeable nation-states, like Apple overtaking Italy in 2020, may begin their own corporate currencies and start to bypass nation-states financially too. Microsoft's WO2020060606 cybercurrency patent and Facebook Libra also suggest this possibility.

Corporations could even become something akin to a new religion. While we joked about Saint William of Seattle earlier, think about the religious-style fervour their products and corporate culture can instil. For example, when Apple releases a new device, queues of fanatics often form outside the shops days beforehand, and many people have a preference for either Android-everything or Apple-everything, choosing only devices belonging to either brand and operating system then being insistent they will never buy the competing mark. The 2013 film 'The Internship,' starring Owen Wilson and Vince Vaughn, was about how two unlikely salesmen joined Google as interns and succeeded against the odds. The message? That the religion is open to all who contribute, regardless of background perhaps. Apple, Google, and Microsoft all have their own remote campuses, offering a large range of services to employees, so they never need to leave the site. This sounds rather similar to the network of medieval monasteries and cathedrals, with priests, monks, and nuns. Think of the power they wielded back then and consider the power corporations wield now. Every day, many of us already stop what we are doing, pause for a moment and check our devices, our heads bowed, mobiles in our upturned palms as we regard their hardware, apps, and websites. Let us pray. In the years ahead, perhaps it's not so ridiculous to wonder if we will physically make pilgrimages to these key religious sites, to pay homage to our new Saints, and gaze upon the relics, be they the Apple

I computer or the Google 1.0 search engine. Especially if these corporations begin issuing their own cybercurrencies and distributing them as alms.

Perhaps the nearest thing to a technology cult saint already is Saint Steven Jobs of Apple. His products have created fervour for years, as witnessed by the strong following that will only buy Apple products like the iPhone, iPad, and Mac. Many devotees have his portrait on their walls, with his inspirational quotes. Hoping and praying, some of his energy, influence, and power will rub off on them in their new home office. Then, he died suddenly in his fifties, still in his prime and amidst more bookable quotations about how illness had modified his outlook on life and money. Apple already has chapels or temples in many city centres, where you can go and pay homage. Even the Apple logo itself is nothing more than an Apple with a huge bite taken out of it, a biblical reference to Adam and Eve. Have we bitten the forbidden technology fruit?

> "The most compelling reason for most people to buy a computer for the home will be to link it to a nationwide communications network. We're just in the beginning stages of what will be a truly remarkable breakthrough for most people - as remarkable as the telephone."
>
> — Steve Jobs

## CONCLUSIONS

While nation-states decline, they have proved the most useful exercise in what rates of extraction the population will endure if they feel they have a say in how things are run. It seems that people are willing to tolerate being **50 Percent a slave**, as long as they get to tick a box every few years, giving them nominal say on what happens to them in the future. Think back to when royalty ran countries without an elected parliament, as dictators. The tax rates they were able to extract were a lot, lot lower. In that respect, nation-states may persist as a front for other powers behind them, the ones really deciding things. 1930s Germany, with the close ties between big industry and politics, is a great example of this and may have become an example for the rest of the world, had they not lost World War Two.

Corporations may take over the issuance and control of money from nation-states. At the very least, it's possible that corporate and government fiat currencies may exist together in the same time frame, but the wealth has migrated away from nation-states, and we may find out more about exactly how much has migrated away if we get there and find the gold and silver vaults empty.

> "Old Mother Hubbard
> Went to the Cupboard,
> To give the poor Dog a bone;
> When she came there,
> The Cupboard was bare,
> And so the poor Dog had none."
>
> — Old English nursery rhyme

Even if large corporations prosper, the US DJIA stock index and gold have a history of a near meeting when a financial crisis bottoms out. Currently, the DJIA is worth around 14 times the price of an ounce of gold. In 1932 and 1980, just over one ounce of gold bought the DJIA. Whether a large stock market crash achieves that, as was the case in

1932, or inflation pushing up the gold price, as was the case in 1980, it may be destined to happen again.

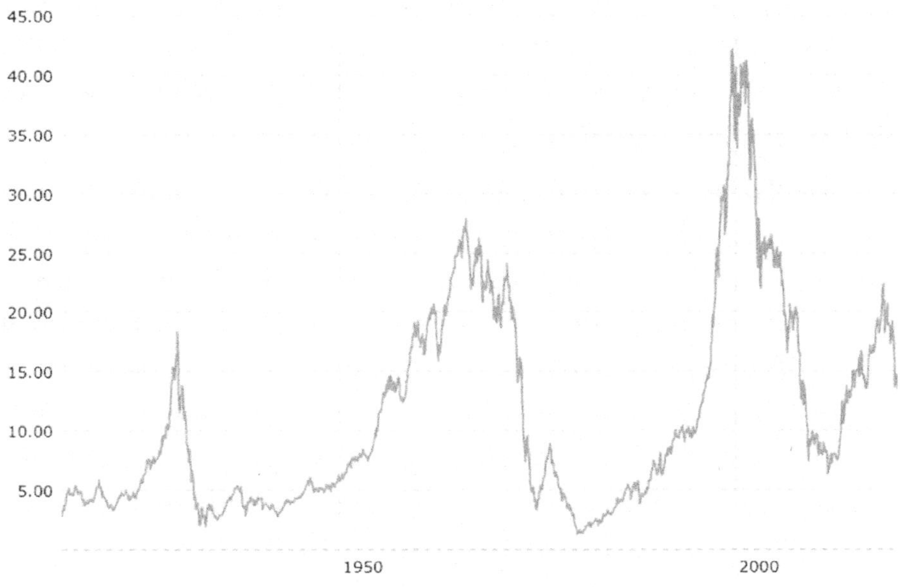

*(Chart: DJIA priced in ounces of gold)*

The incumbent empire at the beginning of the century, usually loses whatever conflict occurs. Great Britain may have felt it won World War 1, and yes, the USA was apparently on the same side, but that war helped expedite the transfer of the true wealth and centre of empire from London to Washington. Even if it wasn't apparent at the time. The British Empire was the largest it had ever been in 1920, but the map hid the weaknesses, a bit like Hitler in 1945, in Berlin, deep underground in a bunker moving phantom armies around on a map to counter the Russian assaults. Looking back, the transfer of wealth behind the scenes always happens, even if the imperial number one of one century continues to prosper to a lesser extent in the new century. Maybe history will be different this time, or maybe it won't? Who can know?

By now, you're probably wondering what countries are safe and which are not. **The Crown** is a clue as to how uncertain this is. Not only were restrictions heavy worldwide, even countries you may have thought of as freer or where state interference was less implemented them. Here are three factors to think about:-

- History shows that the countries that formed the last empire tend to struggle more economically in the new paradigm. While the U.K. partly avoided this fate in the last century, Spain and medieval China suggest the decline can last generations. This would imply the Anglo-Saxon British Empire (U.K., U.S.A., Canada, Australia...) may underperform in the next 100 years, along with other European Union countries like France and Germany, who also have high levels of debt.

- Having access to resources for food, heating, and also potentially profitable resale, either as an individual or within a nation-state, could help.

- Countries with the biggest gold reserves and the lowest debt may perform better economically than those on a desperate asset grab, the ones restricting freedoms everywhere. Often these are countries that did not participate in the economic benefits of the last empire or are considered emerging today. Russia, including former Soviet republics, China, and parts of Africa, may fit into this category.

Again, none of this constitutes certainty or advice. It is mere speculation about how things *could* go in the future.

## SUMMARY

The world is going through a major change. Possibly a whole new era of mankind's history, the technology era. However, the one thing that will almost certainly stay the same is the role of gold behind it all. Gold and silver have always been used as the stored form of savings by civilisations through good times, wars, and natural disasters. They almost certainly will be again. Regardless of what nations and fiat currencies collapse, or what corporate currencies rise. Over the last 110 years, we have lost touch with that and now transact in dubious modern equivalents compared to what our ancestors knew as money. Our ancestors were also freer then; their only state interactions in many cases would've been saying hello to the local policeman or receiving a letter via the postman. For most, there were no taxes to pay and few rules to follow. Community meant something, and most people didn't really need someone to tell them what's right and what's wrong. While we think we're cleverer now, we're more controlled and regulated than many of us seem to realise, and it also has the potential to get a lot, lot worse. If the system isn't going to give you freedom or the gold and silver that has been taken from you, then perhaps you need to find your own ways to regain it. Perhaps one quote needs a modern equivalent:-

"First they came for the Gold,
and I did not speak out—
Because I was told, it was for our own good.
Then they came for the Silver,
and I did not speak out—
Because I was told those with Silver
had earnt it dishonestly.
Then they came for our Freedom,
and I did not speak out—
Because I was certain, I had nothing to hide.
Then they came for me—and there
was no one left to speak for me."

— Adapted from Martin Niemoller

Very few people even own any gold or silver nowadays. Some people have a few old coins of silver and even gold in the drawer, perhaps, but that's about it. Had long-gone family members seen through the conjuring tricks and consciously decided to store them during bad times? A notable exception being India and the Middle East, but even there moves are being made to get more and more people into current mainstream financial thinking. If you do, it's mostly as jewellery, only worn on special occasions, or as a gold wedding ring. The ultimate savings store on your finger in case of a time of extreme crisis. You may need it.

Against this backdrop of uncertainty, along with the clues of what has actually happened in the last 100 years and where that creep into our personal lives has got us, perhaps the best you can do is protect yourself, and those you care about and trust others will do the same. Take care.

# THE WONDERFUL WIZARD OF OZ

"Pay no attention to the man behind the curtain!"

— L. Frank Baum

If you feel a little despondent right now, luckily, it's time for the motivational part. Once upon a time, there was a young girl who, with a few friends she made along the way, exposed the whole financial system as the con it is.

This is, of course, about "The Wizard of Oz."

What, you didn't know the story was an allegory for gold and sound money? It's understandable since no-one ever tells the real meaning behind the story, which dates from 1900.

As you probably know, a young girl, Dorothy, meets a Tin Man, a Scarecrow, and a cowardly Lion. There's major hardship across the land, and she's heard a wizard in a remote place can help save them all. Along the journey, they encounter trials and tribulations, defeating them all, while constantly following this yellow brick road all the way to Oz, where the wizard is found. Sadly he's not actually much of a help with anything, all he ever does is pull a few levers and pretend to be powerful. Reality is, they've all grown and overcome the limiting factors that were stopping them from achieving whatever it was they wished to achieve.

An inspirational story indeed. However, what's lost is the real meaning. The Tin Man and the Scarecrow represent the Industrial worker and the agricultural worker. The Lion, an office worker, and the bravery we've all lost, the fear of pushing ahead and achieving our own dreams. The road to Oz is, of course, the yellow brick road of gold Bars. Oz. being the representative sign for what gold was and still is traded in today, Ounces. When they reach the Emerald City, the Guardian of the Gates distracts them from the Wizard by telling them to go kill the Wicked Witch of the West. Eerily comparable to wars, where citizens are told who is a friend and who is an enemy and sent off to fight them. As World Wars 1 and 2 showed, they often don't come back. In this case, when they return, the wizard behind the curtain, who represents the central bankers playing with the economy, believing they're in control and can create prosperity for everyone, is exposed as a fraud.

The key message - the power is within us, we walk the road of gold bars with every single transaction we decide to make, and no wizard is achieving fantastic magical feats with our money, he's just pulling levers, fooling everyone he's in control, and the sooner we realise that, exposing him for what he is and taking back control, the better.

# FORWARD PLANNING

"Hope for the Best and prepare for the Worst."

— Various sources

By this point, you are probably wondering what you can do to protect yourself and those dear to you.

Some financial publications may recommend you to diversify into owning a second home in a faraway location, a bolthole perhaps. These kinds of expensive choices simply aren't realistic advice for the majority of people, but there are still many small things you can do to give yourself a headstart if things go wrong.

*Note: none of this represents official advice, and you are recommended to make your own decisions in consultation with experts on your particular circumstances.*

## A CASH MINDSET

One of the first is to get back into a cash mindset. This one in itself is hard for many, who have become used to carrying a single credit card or even using Mobile payment apps, then tapping it contactlessly on the credit card machine at the shop. The Corona crisis speeded up another trend. You may remember that if the Machine stops, or bank accounts become harder to access through restrictions, the exchange rate between digital currency you can only see on a screen and physical currency you hold in your hand as notes and coins may change from 1:1 to something much more. In an extreme situation, you could also imagine desperate people outside a shop offering to buy or trade your physical currency to pay for food.

Conversely, governments might outlaw physical cash, as they recently did in India with certain denominations being retired, resulting in a deluge of customers queueing at banks to exchange their soon-to-be worthless banknotes or convert them into digital currency via a bank account. However, even in this example, there was a window of time for you to pay the money back into your account with no loss incurred.

This advice applies even if you continue to pay for goods and services using your electronic methods. The key is to:-

a) Get used to having a usable amount of physical currency on your person at all times again, just in case it is required because electronic payment methods are down

b) Retain an acceptable amount of physical currency in your household, say, one month's worth of expenses. In case of electronic payment unavailability or a banking crisis

Especially when the bank pays you 0% interest anyway, and let's not forget that *contrary to popular opinion, banks do sometimes go bust*. In a way, it's no different from those American pilots and their two gold sovereigns. So just think of yourself as a Top Gun fighter ace, carrying a bit of insurance on your next mission outside of the home.

## STOCK UP

The second step is to stock up on the core commodities important to your life.

The major one of these is food. For example, 100 years ago, the average household spent up to 50% of its income on food. Today, that figure is nearer 10%, giving us all more disposable income for consumer goods, bigger mortgage repayments, and exotic holidays.

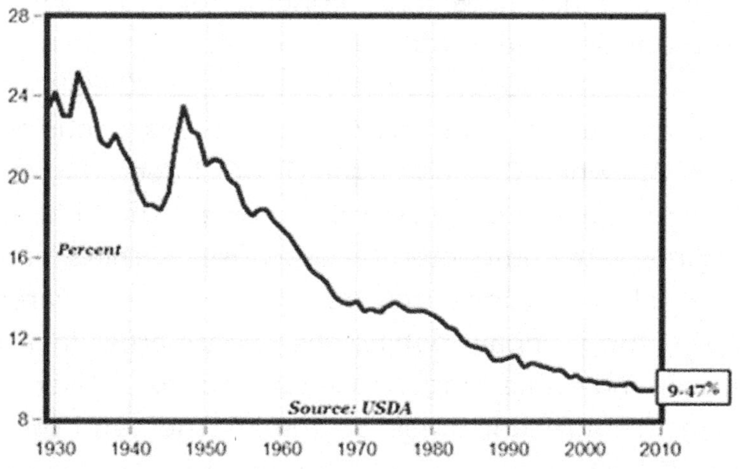


*(Chart showing food prices as a proportion of income)*

Conversely, it has also allowed for a real decline in income, masked by fiat currency inflation, meaning many of us are worse off than ever.

*(Chart showing income versus gold)*

We may well already be being prepared for future food shortages and increases in food prices. You may have already noticed shortages during the crisis or increases. On a personal level, visiting the supermarket regularly, a 20-25% increase in fruit, vegetables, and dairy products has occurred since March 2020, when Corona began. That's interesting, as these products are all the ones with the shortest shelf life, that are most immediately impacted by price rises. Others, like dried, tinned and frozen goods, may be in huge stock at warehouses down the supply chain behind the supermarket facade, and price rises may take longer to feed through. Observe these headlines from recent times, on the internet, and think once more of Edward Bernays and "Propaganda", as to what they may be planting the seed in your head to germinate for:-

"UK potato farmers fear another washout for this year's crop. "

> — The Guardian, August 2020

"Bread price may rise after dire UK wheat Harvest."

> — BBC News, August 2020

"Coronavirus: Meat shortage leaves US farmers with 'mind-blowing' choice."

> — BBC News, May 2020

If you wonder how far prices can rise during a monetary crisis, then here is an example of prices from "Fiat Money Inflation in France," an excellent study of the hyperinflation that occurred there during the French revolutionary times, which coincide with the decline of the French empire before the handover to Great Britain.

|  | 1790 | 1795 |
|---|---|---|
| For a bushel of flour | 40 cents | 45 dollars |
| For a bushel of oats | 18 cents | 10 dollars |
| For a cartload of wood | 4 dollars | 500 dollars |
| For a bushel of coal | 7 cents | 2 dollars |
| For a pound of sugar | 18 cents | 12½ dollars |
| For a pound of soap | 18 cents | 8 dollars |
| For a pound of candles | 18 cents | 8 dollars |
| For one cabbage | 8 cents | 5½ dollars |
| For a pair of shoes | 1 dollar | 40 dollars |
| For twenty-five eggs | 24 cents | 5 dollars |

Now, how well covered are you for those kinds of price rises in basic commodities, the essentials of life?

Clothes are also really cheap right now, as retailers dump tons of unsold stock from the 2020 fashion ranges onto the market at bargain prices. If you already have enough clothes, fine, but if not, it might be a good time to ensure you do, especially clothes to see you through cold winters. With this glut, it's hard to know what will happen to all elements of the clothing supply chain in the future: Cotton farmers, Garment manufacturers, and clothing retailers.

## DIVERSIFY YOUR LIFE AS BEST YOU CAN

While second properties and relocating to the Cayman Islands may be beyond most, there are still diversification strategies you can undertake.

By fortune, many of us will have opportunities to gain the passport of a father or mother in addition to the one you already hold. This is recommended in most cases. Exceptions might be the USA, which taxes all citizens on their worldwide income or controlling governments that demand to know where you are or demand you live by some of their rules, even if you don't live in their country anymore.

Many of us have also already lived or worked in more than one country. Another useful diversification strategy would be to retain any bank accounts in foreign countries that you have and top them up with a small amount of money, just in case. Especially if those accounts have a payment card attached to them.

When it comes to your property or living arrangements, that is entirely up to you. Property prices may fall dramatically in a crisis, but they also have huge potential to rise massively if people are displaced. Crime may rise, and food shortages may occur, but again it's hard to know in advance which regions will be most affected. In an extreme situation, it may be one time where closeness to food supplies and separation from others who are in desperate times matters. In recent history, civilisation has meant cities being preferable and offering more opportunities for culture and growth, as witnessed by the huge migrations from the country to the cities during the Industrial Era. This may be one of the other times where this is not the case. The increase in homeworking in 2020, as a result of **The Crown**, could also see rural locations favoured as no commuting to a central place of work is required anymore by many.

Ultimately, the house you live in should be viewed solely as a commodity - are you happy there, are family and friends close by as a support network, can you afford to live there if you lose your means of income? These are the questions you would ask when buying or selling anyway, and they're the main ones to ask in this case. The other thing about commodities is that you utilise them until they are exhausted. Similarly, some may find they have to do this with their home in the future.

When it comes to Stocks and Shares, Realise that some shares will go up, some will go down. Deflation might destroy the value of many investments you hold. Inflation might also destroy the true value of many investments you hold, but at least the statements might look good, showing a value of, say, £20m, the unfortunate thing being it's enough to buy a loaf of bread. Some businesses stand to do incredibly well out of many of the things mentioned in the threads of this publication. For example, in **Data is the New Oil**.

With your investments, some simple things are recommended.

## DON'T PUT ALL YOUR EGGS IN ONE BASKET

This has historically been an investment maxim for diversification, but could just as easily have been written to mean "Don't put all your savings with one savings institution" and goes right back to the early days of banking. It could even mean you don't put yourself and your life totally in one national basket, lest someone destroys it. With banks, most countries now have a limit below which your savings are 100% protected should something happen to the financial institution in question. Financial institutions are obliged to notify you of these limits in their terms and conditions for the accounts. Anything above the protected level would be completely lost in the event of a crisis, so make sure you are below the limits. In truth, these limits have never really been tested on a national level. Isolated banks have failed, and takeovers and bailouts have been encouraged and engineered, often with the complicity of government. However, it's not a rare event - it almost happened on an international scale back in 2008-09.

The same applies to investments. Instead of one brokerage account with all of your entire holdings, you may be better off holding several brokerage accounts with lower investment levels, just to maximise your protection from a failure of the broker itself.

International diversification may take many forms that do not even become apparent until later. For example, during a recent crisis in Argentina, the government banned the holding of US dollars. Many enterprising Argentinians realised that they could hold US Dollars in their PayPal accounts, where the government could not touch them. Sometimes you may need to think on your feet in an emergency, and these people are a great example of that.

## GET PHYSICAL

No, not the song by Olivia Newton-John. It's a bit like with cash versus digital, have some access to physical gold and silver as the ultimate trading items to survive. Small-denomination coins are best in this case if required for emergency payment of goods and services. Jewellery is also good in this respect.

Nothing in life is guaranteed. If some of the things described here come to pass, it might be unrealistic to avoid the impact. If a train is coming, the best thing you can do is get out of the way well in advance rather than try to face it down and hope it stops before it reaches you. I wish you well with what the future holds for us all.

# MEDIA AND INTERNET

"Right now, there is a whole, an entire generation that never knew anything that didn't come out of this tube. This tube is the gospel, the ultimate revelation; this tube can make or break presidents, popes, prime ministers; this tube is the most awesome goddamn propaganda force in the whole godless world, and woe is us if it ever falls into the hands of the wrong people, and that's why woe is us that Edward George Ruddy died. Because this company is now in the hands of CCA, the Communications Corporation of America, there's a new chairman of the board, a man called Frank Hackett, sitting in Mr. Ruddy's office on the twentieth floor. And when the 12th largest company in the world controls the most awesome goddamn propaganda force in the whole godless world, who knows what shit will be peddled for truth on this network?"

— Howard Beale, from the film Network, 1976

What was predicted in Network has come to pass; 6 big companies now own most of the media in the USA:-

- National Amusements
- Disney
- TimeWarner
- Comcast
- Newscorp
- Sony

Belief and interest in the mainstream TV news had hit an all-time low before **The Crown**. However, now it has become more relevant again, and people are scared; they are turning back in the traditional TV channels, much like people huddled around their radios in wartime, awaiting the latest news from the front. For example, on March 20th, 2020, BBC reported viewing figures of 9 million for the 'Six O'clock News' programme. The highest figure since Christmas 2008 and more than double the 4.2 million average of 2019.

Yet, with corporations owning the media on one side, and the state-funded broadcasting channels, such as the BBC on the other, who is truly independent?

Here are three recent examples of media manipulation, either accidental or possibly not.

- US news channel CBS broadcast footage of a hospital in New York during the height of the Coronavirus in April 2020. Eagle-eyed viewers spotted the footage was the same as footage as previously shown elsewhere from Italy, and CBS was forced to apologise.

- In the 1990 gulf war, a girl called 'Nayirah' gave testimony to US Congress that Iraqi troops murdered babies in Kuwait after the Iraq invasion. This story was used to win support and justify the invasion by the

US later. Even Amnesty International confirmed the story to be true. TV News and newspapers worldwide covered it all enthusiastically. The problem? 'Nayirah' was actually the daughter of the Kuwaiti ambassador to the United States, and it was all a lie. Only exposed well after the war ended, and the story had served its purpose.

- BBC broadcast footage in 2018 of a hospital in Douma, Syria, supposedly full of victims of a chemical attack. BBC Producer Riam Dalati even said himself later publicly that he believed the footage was 'staged.'

Going back to 1910, there is no doubt newspapers had a lot of power in influencing the population. The 1914 stories in the UK newspapers of German soldiers murdering Belgian babies in their hospital beds sounds weirdly similar to the story with Iraqis murdering Kuwaiti babies back in 1991. Both subsequently proven well after the alleged events to have been fake. Then how about the Lusitania, sunk in the Atlantic by a German U-boat in 1915, the incident that was used to help stir the USA into joining the fight against the Hun? You know, that terrible sinking of a harmless passenger ship, with the loss of 1,193 innocent civilians? Well, what was never reported at the time was that the Lusitania had a false bill of lading and was carrying munitions. The Germans knew this and even posted a newspaper advert saying it might be sunk if it sailed. A fact conveniently hidden and only finally admitted in the 1980s when a salvage company announced it was planning to explore the wreck. Within the corridors of power, this caused huge concern that there could be a massive explosion if they were allowed to do so, so the truth had to be told.

NOTICE!

TRAVELLERS intending to embark on the Atlantic voyage are reminded that a state of war exists between Germany and her allies and Great Britain and her allies; that the zone of war includes the waters adjacent to the British Isles; that, in accordance with formal notice given by the Imperial German Government, vessels flying the flag of Great Britain, or of any of her allies, are liable to destruction in those waters and that travellers sailing in the war zone on ships of Great Britain or her allies do so at their own risk.

IMPERIAL GERMAN EMBASSY

WASHINGTON, D. C., APRIL 22, 1915.

Perhaps the words of an ex-US president, written 200 years ago, but as relevant as ever, say it best:-

"I will add, that the man who never looks into a newspaper is better informed than he who reads them; in as much as he who knows nothing is nearer to the truth than he whose mind is filled with falsehoods & errors. He who reads nothing will still learn the great facts, and the details are all false."

— Thomas Jefferson, 1800s

Jefferson has been proved right, even in the modern era. The omission by media of the USA reducing the Reserve Lending ratio to zero, mentioned in **The Crown**, is an excellent example of how media-dominating events like Corona can help what would be major stories on any other day to go unreported. On September 10th, 2001, Donald Rumsfeld announced that the C.I.A could not account for up to $2.3

Trillion in missing funds. This major story got lost amongst events on September 11th, 2001, at the World Trade Centre. On that day, a Labour spin doctor in the UK, Jo Moore, also sent a memo around at 2.54 pm, as the events unfolded, saying, "It is now a very good day to get out anything we want to bury." Sometimes the news you don't see is more important than that you are presented with.

Accept that television is often like watching an illusionist conduct a magic trick. While watching, you become sucked into the illusion, the production values are superb, and the results magnificent, drawing up emotions within you. You have no idea who the stooges or the unwitting audience members tricked into participating were and what sleights-of-hand occurred. In fact, it's only much later that you begin to think about any of those things, and by then, it's passed. It was just a bit of fun anyway; the audience member normally gets their wallet or £10 note back in one piece, no harm done. Whereas a magic show can be excellent escapism, these media conjuring tricks can be attempts to buy your complicity in gigantic thefts *from you*. Why not try cutting off the supply, even for a day or two, and see how you feel? Imagine yourself as Thomas Jefferson, who was neither a fan of the media nor a fan of big banking interests.

It's up to you, ultimately, whether you will continue watching or not, of course. Perhaps, if you do, try to watch the programmes with a more critical eye and listen for the words that emotionally trigger you. After all, if you haven't witnessed something for yourself or no-one in your network has been personally affected by it, is it provably true and relevant to your life? Remember - it's not just the news; as mentioned, many places in this publication, the internet, films, and TV shows are also planting ideas and thoughts in our minds. It's not even a new thing, for it's exactly what Edward Bernays in 'Propaganda' explained was happening, way back in 1928.

If you continue watching, then the Channel 4 TV shows by Derren Brown can also be a most interesting watch in respect of understanding how much our minds can be controlled and our morality can be tested. In one episode, 'The Push,' he demonstrates how someone can be gradually psychologically manipulated into committing a murder.

## INTERNET

Has the power to influence got less? Probably not. Newspapers have definitely declined, so have books, but now we spend much of our life watching TV and online. The internet is now also where the influence is. Advertising spend has increasingly moved online to the likes of Google and Facebook, as old media wanes. Aside from its immense power as the new main advertising media, many are already reporting that the advertising they are presented with seems suspiciously well-focussed. In fact, some people don't even remember interacting with a computer about certain things they talked about or thought about buying. Yet the adverts seem rather *too* relevant.

The internet also has incredible power to influence your moods. Facebook even admitted an experiment in 2012 to test its power to influence user moods. Without them even knowing, users were presented with good or bad stories, preferring to other stories they might have viewed instead. Not just a few users, but Facebook said '700,000 English-speaking users', whose feeds were skewed to either be happier or sadder than normal. Even now, it's not known which users were affected, and they have no idea they were part of the experiment. As the saying goes, 'if something is free, you are the product.' At the very least, let's make the results public for us all to see.

Bearing in mind that *Data is The New Oil*, the data-gathering possibilities from these sites is huge. Of course, these sites add value, and no-one is saying don't use them but have some restraint. There have been stories of property vandalism from teenage house party posts that went viral online, burglaries where people posted they were on holiday, and of course, even just logging in or having the apps on your phone usually means you're gifting them your location, shopping and transportation data. Just delve into your Google account and see their history of your past physical activities. Unless you have opted out, you may be surprised.

So perhaps the main thing to remember is *Don't feed the machine*. Every day we gift our devices so much information. It's impossible to avoid in reality, because we need to communicate and transact. However, think about old accounts you don't use anymore and think twice when websites ask you for extra information, such as a mobile phone number, whether they have a valid need for that information. It may even pay to have secondary, disposable email addresses for signing up to some websites.

To get around some of this tracking and intrusion into your privacy and personal life, you may wish to consider a VPN.

## VIRTUAL PRIVATE NETWORK (VPN)

For your own security and privacy, a VPN solution may be a help. This has the effect of masking your true location on many websites. Where it can be useful, however, is to overcome censorship or cross-border restrictions.

For example, since 2016, when the European Union implemented new internet regulations, many US news websites are no longer accessible from the EU, as the website owners do not wish to take on the burden of the regulations. This has had the effect of less freedom of information, even if that were not the intention. A VPN is a perfect way around this.

Another example is website restrictions - for example, your internet banking, or even Facebook, may be blocked when you are visiting another country. In an extreme situation, this could leave you much stranded from a virtual point of view. Again, a VPN can help present you as being in your normal home country and access the services you need to access.

Some people often naively believe 'I have nothing to hide.' That may be true, but in a time of crisis, how would you feel if, despite believing you have nothing to hide, your government locks down your ability to talk to family members abroad or access your own money? These things already happen in certain countries and can fairly easily be implemented anywhere, should a government wish to do so.

At the time of writing, there are even free VPN services, although these often get negative coverage for using your internet connection for other data transfer. Paid for services are available for as little as a few pounds a month. It pays to research carefully before committing to a particular provider.

## MOBILE PHONE

In the USA, a social security number is a unique identifier with privacy protection rights are written in the law, a mobile phone number has no such privacy protection rights, and people tend to hand them over willy-nilly, without thinking of possible consequences.

Think again about doing so. You may not have realised it, but your mobile number is your new unofficial social security number, recognised internationally. Imagine that the unique identifying key for you, used by a multitude of IT systems without you even knowing. Sometimes they may even share this information with other organisations, depending on what you signed up to in the terms and conditions that few of us ever read, just ticking the box to move on.

**Data is the New Oil** mentioned the increased data gathering taking place right now. Now, does it make sense why so many websites and data capture services request this piece of information about you? In 2020, the European Union introduced new '2-step' authentication laws for finance and access to banking services. Now, in many cases, it's no longer possible to access accounts or do transactions without submitting a working mobile number. Are they doing this to protect you, or are they doing it to improve tracking of the population? Who knows?

It may be hard to accept, but perhaps change your mobile number occasionally and never become too attached to a certain number. Hard to face for some, and of course, this recommendation accepts that if the powers that be are really looking for you, '...they will hunt you down and they will find you...' to paraphrase Liam Neeson, in the film 'Taken.' Just think about it this way, why does that airline you last flew with 5 years ago, the website you don't use anymore or the internet bank account with the zero balance you'll never use again need to know the current live information about you? This is the problem with a mobile; it's been identified as the one piece of unique key data that people retain for a long time, way more than even living in the same address - one of the previous main identifiers.

## SUMMARY

We will again turn to the 1976 film, 'Network,' in which a TV presenter, played by Howard Beale, starts telling it exactly how it really is. Initially, the studio tries to shut him down and get him off-air, but he proves such a rating hit, with his seemingly insane rants that they leave him on. Temporarily at least, people listen to him and act on his recommendations.

"I don't have to tell you things are bad. Everybody knows things are bad. It's a depression. Everybody's out of work or scared of losing their job. The dollar buys a nickel's worth. Banks are going bust. Shopkeepers keep a gun under the counter. Punks are running wild in the street, and there's nobody anywhere who seems to know what to do, and there's no end to it. We know the air is unfit to breathe and our food is unfit to eat, and we sit watching our TVs while some local newscaster tells us that today we had fifteen homicides and sixty-three violent crimes, as if that's the way it's supposed to be.

We know things are bad – worse than bad. They're crazy. It's like everything everywhere is going crazy, so we don't go out anymore. We sit in the house, and slowly the world we live in is getting smaller, and all we say is: 'Please, at least leave us alone in our living rooms. Let me have my toaster and my TV and my steel-belted radials, and I won't say anything. Just leave us alone.'

Well, I'm not gonna leave you alone. I want you to get MAD! I don't want you to protest. I don't want you to riot – I don't want you to write to your congressman because I wouldn't know what to tell you to write. I don't know what to do about the depression and the inflation and the Russians and the crime in the street. All I know is that first, you've got to get mad. (Shouting) You've got to say: 'I'm a human being, god-dammit! My life has value!"

— Howard Beale, from the film Network, 1976

Considering that it was written 44 years ago, it's amazing that everything is still relevant today, including the depression, inflation, and being further isolated in our homes.

In the final part of this book, we look at possibly better, safer forms of currency. Some of them we are losing or have lost but may benefit from turning back to before it is too late.

# COMMUNITY CURRENCY

"I alone cannot change the world, but I can cast a stone across the waters to create many ripples."

— Mother Teresa

It's time to get back into the mindset that our bodies and minds are the best sources of currency and wealth generation going, no implant for cryptocurrency earning required. It's always been so. People thousands of years ago knew that if they wished to generate wealth and transact to get what they wanted from life, it meant using the assets they have - whether it meant fishing, chopping down a tree for firewood, or digging a field and planting some seeds - it all led to productive situations where they could enhance their own lives and make their own trades on mutually beneficial terms with fellow humans.

Yet, we seem to have forgotten that. Many of us have lost our independence and power without even realising it and have no idea how to get it back. It's not a surprise; a hundred years of history has seen us separated from the reality of the medium of exchange we use between us, from something trustworthy, with value, to paper, then digital. As if that wasn't enough, the freedom to live our lives, however, we choose got taken away too, with rules and regulations to follow instead, with rewards for following the 'right' behaviour and punishments or, at the very least, making it impossible to live the life you want to. That's what the welfare state and tax law, with breaks and exemptions for certain behaviours. Some of these tax exemptions aren't even something a normal person could ever hope to take advantage of - for example, donating to your own charitable foundation that you can then control the distribution of tax-free funds from.

The importance of community has also disappeared on the journey through the Twentieth century and into now. As an example of the importance of community, a story in Bernard Lietauer's "The Future of Money" sums this up pretty well. Imagine one day you decide to go to the shop to buy some nails for a fence. On your way there, you encounter a neighbour and talk about the purpose of your trip. On hearing about the nails, the neighbour tells you that he has some leftover from his own fence repairs last year that you are welcome to have. You take them, and both leave happy; you got the nails you needed, and a transaction of mutual trust took place. You're more likely to wave to each other next time you see each other, look out for each other's property if someone is away, and help each other out should the need arise again.

What just happened there is exactly what the system doesn't want, because there's nothing in it for them. It can't be measured in pure fiat currency. Had you gone to the hardware shop and made a purchase in your national currency, there would've been a sales tax cut for the government, an income or corporation tax cut on the retailer and manufacturer profits, and an increase in GDP, always used as a measure of the success of a country. The community version of the transaction may also be a real win-win for the environment, too, maximising usage of available resources and minimising waste - the nails might've just rusted away and not even been ultimately used at all.

GDP in itself is a problematic figure anyway, as it assumes all economic activity is worthwhile. Which it is not. Frederic Bastiat's broken window theory best sums this up - he proposed, as a joke way back in the 1790s, that the economic activity of nations could be increased by breaking windows. A bonanza for economic activity, glaziers especially, but not anything that improves the general human condition. In fact, paying for the broken glass repair would be likely to mean a deferral of other more beneficial economic activity. No matter, the GDP figures would look good.

Denmark, for example, even has childcare rules around this, where a paid childcarer cannot care for their own child, only other children. Their own child must be placed with another carer, who then gets paid for looking after him/her. You may even question other aspects of this rule, but on a basic level, it helps GDP rise without adding anything.

Whether post-world War 2 city planners intended it to be so or not, the compulsory purchase and demolition of older terraced housing in the UK, plus the destruction of traditional industry in the 1980s, has led to a forced dispersal of people and a loss of community and with it, transactions of the nail type. Nowadays, we are unlikely to know the people living in the same street as us, which often feeds suspicion and dislike or irritation with neighbours instead of community spirit. This trend has fed through into the online sphere, where Facebook comments stating a different opinion often generate a lot of spiteful and hateful replies that people would never make to each other in person. The internet has allowed people to become desensitised to each other, a concept explored in the TV series "Black Mirror", with the episode "Hated in the Nation."

Yet community currency could mean so much more. In some places, there have been localised attempts to formalise community currency, creating a complementary currency that works alongside the national fiat. In these systems, people could state their fees in community currency for a service and be paid in it. Then, use up those saved community currency units to pay others locally for services they require. 'Ithaca Hours,' a community currency in New York, USA, was a good example, but as these rely on the goodwill and hard work of a few people, they tend to fade away over time. Certainly, as technology gets cheaper to manage such systems, there may be other examples appearing in the future. The government does not help in many cases, by being suspicious of such systems and even outright closing them down sometimes, since, going back to the nail example, it is no longer collecting the income and sales taxes it gets from fiat currency transactions.

Therein probably lies the main problem. Should individual citizen transactions even be taxed at all? If you think the concept of no income tax is ridiculous, then bear in mind, it's exactly how most of the world operated before World War 2 and especially World War 1. When the US Federal Reserve was formed in 1913, very few people paid income tax, and those that did would be classed as very rich by today's standards. Compare it to now where virtually everyone is sucked into the income tax system, seeing a large portion of their earnings disappear before they even receive it. Even people on very low incomes fall into the income tax trap in most nation-states. Not only do taxes burden every individual transaction, but they also lead to the gradual hoovering of wealth from the local, community level to a central location. This central location then has the power to distribute and spend this collected wealth as it sees fit, often leading to the gradual impoverishment and decline of certain communities and areas compared to others, based on rules they get to define.

Returning to **Data is The New Oil** briefly, we can wonder if imposing income taxes on even the lowest incomes is about tax revenues or more about data gathering and surveillance.

No-one is saying that community currency can take over the world. It is, however, a very useful tool in encouraging many of the positive aspects of humanity and the community to come back. What's also important is that people return to the freedom to transact with others on their own terms and without interference from outside entities. This is, sadly, lacking in today's world.

It may even get worse. In addition to cryptocurrency implants, we may have to face a new currency called social credits. Increasingly, everything we do is being recorded online, and Facebook, for example, can gain an incredibly accurate view of your likes and dislikes, political affiliations, and likely views on any given subject just by analysing your profile information and past interactions. Imagine if your Facebook/ Twitter comments or public actions were rated by others, or the state as being good or bad, or even that you were rated on the associations you had with others deemed undesirable by the community? In a way, this is a dystopian form of community currency, as your neighbours and people could even get to decide over you and what you can or can't do in life and was also explored in another episode of "Black Mirror", "Nosedive." It's a form of community currency, but instead of being a community currency based on co-operation and mutual advantage, the lifeblood of any positive transaction, it's a community currency based on competitiveness and hate, where someone is trying to gain an advantage at the expense of another human being.

This is a suggestion of how life could improve, but it's also a warning - community currency is coming, but watch out for which one we get.

# BITCOIN AND DIGITAL CURRENCY

"I think the internet is going to be one of the major forces for reducing the role of government. The one thing that's missing but that will soon be developed is a reliable e-cash."

— Milton Friedman

Since 2007, a new kid on the block appeared with regard to currencies. *Bitcoin*. Actually, while it did, so did hundreds of similar currencies. Many with interesting names and vague backgrounds. For some, performance versus fiat currency has been terrible; for others, it has been spectacular.

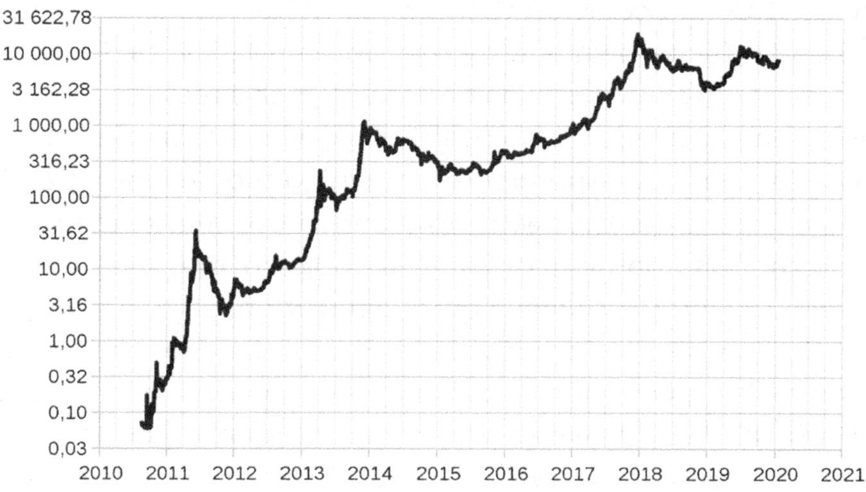



*(Chart: Bitcoin versus USD) - Source: Wikipedia By en: user: Ladislav Mecir, CC BY-SA 3.0)*

It's an alien concept that a currency that exists only electronically can have value. In reality, you get to thinking there must be something behind it of value, something meaning that it is worth something. However, suspend belief for a moment and then think about how most of your fiat currency units exist only in digital form when you make electronic payments and log into your internet banking account. Not only that, but they took the gold backing away and can create as many units as they like. In one way, Bitcoin beats government fiat currencies, which have no limitation on creation, by being limited to 21,000,000 units maximum in circulation. It is also backed by something - *expended electrical power*. That sounds so bizarre that it is well worthy of explanation.

Bitcoins are mined by computers. The computers themselves expend electrical power in mining the coins. It's become so lucrative to mine bitcoins - the logical ones, waiting to be mined and not yet in circulation, that is, hackers are hacking into IT systems simply to use the processing power to mine coins on their behalf. When the alternative is expending your own energy that you must pay for, finding a 'free' energy source is a major benefit. In this respect, Bitcoins bear some similarity to gold and silver, where there are energy and fiat currency expenditures in mining the precious metals. The difference is that with gold and silver, the mined metal represents something physical to hold in the vault as the wealth behind the tokens now in circulation.

Bitcoin also fits other criteria of sound money that makes it more like a community currency - two people can transact using it, 100% by their own choice, and without any interference by a third party. The downside? You'll need to find people on the other side of the equation willing to accept your Bitcoins as payment. One day the same may be true of fiat currency, but in theory, at least, the same should never be true of gold- or silver-backed currency since a seller will accept it based on receiving a payment in the underlying precious metal.

In summary, it's difficult to see the appeal, and I wish I did because investing around the time of writing the 2007 book would've made a Bitcoin investor very rich. What is understandable is that the currency is decentralised and, therefore, outside the immediate reach of a higher power, such as government, to control it. The other thing that could be of value long term is the unique ownership of the currency units. As long as the transaction trail is available and uniqueness is confirmed, there can be no question of the coins existing in multiple places simultaneously. Fiat currency, with its many ways of creating inflation, does not have this built-in restraint.

However, if everything were valued based on energy expended, then old furniture would be valuable, as some obviously took many hours of work by true craftsmen. Instead, they can often be found in flea markets for giveaway prices. The same goes for many other old items. Secondly, if your computer hard drive or device, or the internet itself no longer works, does the wealth still exist? There have been stories of people who had Bitcoins stored on a computer for years when they were worth next to zero, forgot about them, and then realised years later their new value was huge. The problem? The device with the coins on it was now gone. Compare this to gold and silver, where lost coins still exist *somewhere*, or if you have the coins on your person in the event of an internet or power outage, you can still indulge in face-to-face transactions in your community.

If one day, a cybercurrency became backed by gold and silver somehow, then we should take note and adjust our investment philosophy accordingly. Meanwhile, if you want to invest, please go ahead - maybe in this respect, I'm just a financial dinosaur. Milton Friedman did say 'reliable.' Perhaps digital currency can be considered in that way, as one of several 'wallets,' of both virtual and physical types, that we are all going to maintain in the future and make conscious decisions on which works best in any given transaction.

# GOLD AND SILVER INVESTING

"Because gold is honest money, it is disliked by dishonest men."

— Ron Paul

Now we'll look at the other essential factor to consider in protecting your stored savings in a future crisis - saving at least some in gold and silver. In one way, it can be seen as exchanging your fiat currency back into the form that it was in way back in 1910, as described at the beginning.

There are a variety of methods available.

## GOLD AND SILVER COINS

Physical coins, even just a few, also offer good protection outside of the mainstream financial world, and as most of the major nations were part of the Gold Standard, which ended after World War 1 (1918), there are a huge variety of gold Coins available to collectors and gold investors. Silver coins can often be purchased by weight, priced according to their silver content.

These gold coins were produced by many different nations and can be in high demand with collectors; hence their value can vary over the underlying gold metal. The great thing for anyone buying these kinds of gold coins, not just numismatists (coin collectors), is the fact of holding a piece of real history, of everlasting value, in your hand.

In addition, many gold producing countries like South Africa, Australia, and Canada still produce new gold and silver coins of standard weights.

Gold coins, in particular, are rarely made from solid (or 24 carat) gold. This is because gold is, despite its value and inert properties, a soft metal that can scratch or damage fairly easily. To increase the wear of coins, they were traditionally mixed in an alloy with another metal such as copper. For example, Gold sovereigns are 90% gold.

The same goes for silver coins as with gold, although as silver is of much lower value, these normally constituted the smaller value coins in circulation. These are even easier to find than gold Coins and remained in use for a much longer period. For example, if you have any old British Shillings dated before 1947, these contain silver instead of Nickel.

The great thing about silver coins is that they can often be bought for less than the silver value weight of the coins. This is often true of the base, low-value coins of yesteryear, where millions were originally minted.

## ADVANTAGES OF GOLD AND SILVER COINS

- As standard coins, they are of easily recognisable, documented weight, and value.

- They are small, portable forms of wealth that are easily carried on your person in a time of crisis.

- Physical possession of gold and silver coins is the ultimate way of retaining your wealth. Only theft (governmental or otherwise) can take your wealth from you.

- Gold and Old silver coins in the European Union do not attract VAT.

- Good news for British investors is that expert opinion is that the sale of gold Sovereigns does not attract Capital Gains Tax (CGT) either. This is not something the Inland Revenue would be keen to advertise but because Sovereigns have a face value of One Pound and, therefore, still qualify as currency of the realm. They, therefore, hold huge advantages for British Investors. The same may be true for buying face value gold coinage in the currency of whatever country you live in, although you need to check these rules for yourself, as they can change swiftly.

## DISADVANTAGES OF GOLD AND SILVER COINS

- Premiums are often higher than other forms of investment outlined later

- Physical possession could make you a target for theft so remember to find a safe hiding place

- New silver coins can attract VAT in the European Union, and if so, should be avoided

- When you come to sell, it might be hard to find a willing buyer close to the underlying metal price – your coin dealer will offer a similar percentage under the gold price to what he charged you over the gold price unless your coins are also desirable to collectors.

In summary, visit a reputable coin dealer to make sure you are getting coins worth the money and that you do not pay too much over the underlying value of the metal in the coin. Tell him you are mainly interested in the metal value and not the numismatic element. In this respect, British Sovereigns and South African Krugerrands often seem to have fairly low percentage premiums above the gold value and are universally recognised coins.

Your own government may sometimes also bring out special "limited edition" coin sales that might even include gold bullion coins. These should normally be avoided because the premiums above the underlying metal prices are usually very high. You can often visit coin dealers directly later to purchase the same or similar coins at much lower premiums. You can always use the internet to check if they are a good deal against published coin dealer prices.

Auction sites like eBay are not particularly recommended since you have no way of verifying a sellers' claim until after you have handed your money over. The prices attained on the internet right now also seem rather high considering the additional risks of not having seen or examined the items beforehand and possible postal loss.

Conversely, eBay might turn out to be a good place to sell your coins if there is ever a crisis in the future, and gold is suddenly in great demand again because you can advertise to a worldwide audience at a very low cost.

It is also possible to buy coins from many specialist dealers on the internet, but remember to check out the commissions you'll be paying, insured postage costs, and also whether you'll be liable for customs fees on delivery.

Finally, remember what was said earlier about the US air force pilots and their standard-issue two gold sovereigns. This surely tells us something about the value of owning gold coins in a time of crisis.

## GOLD AND SILVER BARS

These have a lot of the advantages and disadvantages of Coins, such as physically owning the metal. Bars are made in various sizes and can be as convenient to own as the coins, but there are some other factors to consider.

### ADVANTAGES OF GOLD AND SILVER BARS

- Bullion bars are usually available for really low premiums above the gold or silver price.

- Bullion bars can be easily identified and valued, as they are usually hallmarked

- Gold bars do not attract VAT in the EU.

### DISADVANTAGES OF GOLD AND SILVER BARS

- Silver bars do attract VAT in the EU. No EU investor should consider investing in silver bars because of this rule.

- A bullion bar cannot be split into smaller units for trading or payment.

The same dealer who can sell you coins can normally also sell bullion bars on the same basis. It is also possible to buy bullion bars from many specialist dealers on the internet, but remember to check out the commissions you'll be paying, insured postage costs, and also whether you'll be liable for customs fees on delivery.

There are other pitfalls with gold and silver bars if you decide to hold them personally:-

- Where will you store them safely?

- If you decided to cash them in at some change, they might need to re-assayed to test the metal purity, probably at your expense.

## JEWELLERY

Historically, the wearing of jewellery probably comes largely from the need to carry your stored wealth with you, be it in the form of rings, necklaces, or whatever.

Now, since jewellery is the precious metal item most advertised as a certain number of carats, this seems like a good time to explain what a carat is. It is a measure of gold purity, between 1 and 24, where 24 is the highest quality purity. So, if an item is 24-carat gold, it is over 99% gold, about as close to pure gold as it is possible to get. If it is 18-carat, it is 75%, 12-carat means 50%, and 9-carat means 37.5% gold. Many coins are, like gold sovereigns, for example, 90% gold and therefore 22-carat, and hence the different gold hues associated with the different levels of purity, as the rest is made up of base metals. What this means, in reality, is that if you have, for example, a 9-carat gold ring, you should weigh it then multiply the weight by 0.375 to obtain the weight of gold it contains. You can then multiply this by the daily price for gold given in most newspapers to get the approximate value of the ring if you were to sell it today. You might be shocked at how little some of your favourite items are underlyingly worth compared to how much you paid for them.

As silver is much less valuable, silver items are normally of much higher purity. However, pure silver is still too soft for jewellery, and thus, jewellery is normally made of silver alloys like *Sterling Silver*. Sterling silver is 92.5% silver, with the balance made up of another metal, usually copper, to increase the resilience.

Most jewellery in Europe and the USA is worth a lot less than the retail prices in the shops. If gold and silver even came into demand again, you could probably imagine customers at retail stores no longer taking sales assistants at face value when they say such and such item is "18-carat", for example, and asking them detailed questions about how much it weighs and what the precious metal content actually is.

Other regions, such as the Middle East and India, place far more emphasis on the actual precious metals value of the jewellery. It is only conjecture, but perhaps they have more recent examples of financial crises in their histories, making them more aware of the inherent value of such items. Dubai, for example, is said by some to be a good place to buy high-quality gold jewellery at fairly small premiums above the underlying precious metal value.

Second-hand jewellery can sometimes be a good deal. If you know what you are buying and have some form of a comeback, if you are misled on the precious metal content and weight. *Caveat Emptor* or buyer beware.

The major factor in favour of jewellery is that you can wear it. Wearing your wealth so it can be carried easily on your person may be a necessity someday, just as it has been in history before. It may even survive through the modern tradition of giving gold rings at weddings. After all, what is a gold ring carried on the finger but the ultimate last resort item for trade and payment in an emergency?

## STORING YOUR GOLD AND SILVER SAFELY

It may be possible for you to visit your bank and say you wish to purchase gold or silver, and they can arrange a deal. But watch the terms of the deal closely.

It may also be possible for your bank to arrange storage of any physical gold you already own in a safe deposit box.

When it comes to gold storage, there are two forms of ownership to take into account, and the difference between these two forms of ownership is vital, as they could mean the difference between something and nothing in the event of a crisis.

*Allocated Storage*

The gold belongs to you, and the bank is only acting as an agent holding it on your behalf. If you really want your bank to manage a gold investment for you, then it needs to be held like this because it's the only way you are protected if the bank collapses.

*Unallocated Storage*

You only bought a share in the banks' gold. This is not desirable since the bank still has the rights over the gold, and you are only another creditor of the bank. The bank can freely sell that gold in an emergency to pay its creditors, including you (join the queue!).

## ADVANTAGES OF BANK STORAGE

- Could be a fair deal, depending on the fees.

- Depending on what the future holds, it could be safer than storing them at your home

## DISADVANTAGES OF BANK STORAGE

- A bank's primary business nowadays is the issuing of currency, not managing gold. They will charge yearly storage fees for holding your gold.

- In 1933, when the USA confiscated all the nations' gold, where was the first place they looked? That's right, in bank safety deposit boxes. It was even made illegal to open a bank safety deposit box without a warden present.

- If your gold is unallocated, then a bank collapse is a disaster, but even if it's not, would you trust an organisation in this state to safely guard your gold? Consider further that bank collapses normally accompany the inflationary situations that make gold a desirable asset to own.

An alternative is a storage option of your own choice, be it a hidden safe in your home or even a hole in the ground. Archaeological gold and silver hoards dating from hundreds or thousands of years ago are probably evidence of the crises our ancestors had to face and the lengths they had to go to guard their wealth.

Fortunately, compared to our ancestors, we now have many more options to safeguard our wealth by linking at least some of our investments to gold and silver. These investments can often protect your wealth outside of your local government jurisdiction, which can be another useful factor in their favour. So we will now be looking at the paper and electronic forms of gold and silver.

## INVESTMENT FUNDS AND MINING STOCKS

If you have a financial advisor advising you on your investments and you mentioned a gold/silver angle, he would likeliest mention investing in a gold or Natural Resources fund, but you need to be aware that this usually really means a fund investing in mining companies. Merrill Lynch Gold Unit Trust, for example, has magnificent performance figures over prior years, but much of this fund is invested in gold mining companies and not gold itself. This introduces many extra variables into the game and the higher fund management fees that you will be paying.

To minimise these fees, you could then decide to invest directly into mining stocks listed on the stock market yourself, and as the two investment forms are very similar, we will consider them together.

Well, in addition to worrying about the price of the underlying commodity, you have to ask the same business questions you would ask of any other corporation, e.g., is the company well-run? Are the countries in which the mines operate free and open, or could the mines be confiscated? Is the mine environmentally conscious, or are campaigners trying to get it closed down?

Yes, if you pick the right mining companies who discover huge reserves of gold or silver, then the price of these stocks will rise dramatically more than underlying commodity prices, but the simple fact to remember is that you are investing in stocks. As famous author Mark Twain once allegedly commented, "A mine is a hole in the ground with a liar at the top." It is possible to make huge profits in mining companies, but you really need to do your homework.

Another thing to be aware of when investing stocks, especially gold stocks, is "production hedging." In practice, this means the selling of future mining production that has not yet been dug out of the mine, at a price acceptable to both parties, based on today's gold price.

In a falling gold price market, this could be a spectacularly profitable decision, but in a rising gold price market, a really bad business decision has been made because you are forced to sell your production at yesterday's much lower price. The key thing to realise is that this is another business factor that could affect your investment value. The solution? Always look for "unhedged" mining companies.

On the Stock Market, small mining companies in particular also often suffer from wide bid-offer spreads. In case you're not sure what the bid-offer spread is, this is when a share price is listed in the newspaper as being, say, 9p per share, but when you come to buy, the price is 9.25p, and when you come to sell, you are offered 8.75p. It occurs because the Market Maker is buying and selling these shares, making a profit by quoting a lower price to those wanting to sell their shares to him, and a higher price to those wanting to buy from him.

The bid/offer spread is one of the least understood parts of investing and hence one of the sneakiest ways for you to lose money without realising it. Only buy or sell when the bid/offer spread is tight - IE there is not much percentage difference between the selling price and buying price because then you know you are getting a fair deal. It is not uncommon to see shares (especially penny mining shares) listed at, say, 1.25p to sell, and 2.5p to buy. This is a disaster transaction to be avoided at all costs - the share needs to double for you to get your money back, which doesn't even include other fees.

If you do fancy investing in mining stocks, then there are plenty of experts out there who produce newsletters with investing recommendations and who have proven successful track records along with great knowledge on the mining nuances of terms such as "provable resources" and the cost calculations involved in getting ore out of the ground and processed. So, if you are interested, then you should do some research yourself to find a newsletter that suits you and ride on the back of one of these heavyweights.

The one caveat to this would be investing in a miner such as the world's largest mining companies, BHP Billiton and Rio Tinto. Large mining companies are hugely diversified operations with many streams of income from various commodities (even a gold mining company will produce silver and copper as by-products) and various mines worldwide, so are not so affected by one bad decision or unforeseen circumstance in any one area. Okay, performance is unlikely to be so heart-stopping as it would be with a small miner either, but it depends on your own investing aims.

Mining stocks are listed on many stock exchanges throughout the world, especially the USA, Australia, Canada, South Africa, and, more latterly, the London AIM (Alternative Investment Market).

## ADVANTAGES OF GOLD MINING STOCKS

- Direct investing in mining companies gives you geared returns on the gold price increase. For example, if a miner makes $20 profit per ounce when gold is priced at $600, all other things being equal, he will make $40 profit per ounce if gold rises to $620. What other business can double profits like that?

- Mining companies could discover new reserves that boost company value too

- Investment funds are very diversified and give you more diversified coverage than you could ever attain investing on your own account

- Investing in foreign-listed gold mining stocks can put your wealth outside of local government jurisdiction

## DISADVANTAGES OF GOLD MINING STOCKS

- The geared returns can work both ways – a fall in mineral prices can wipe out profitability altogether.

- Mining companies are subject to business or political variances outside of gold and silver prices.

- Direct investment into one or two companies does not give you a very diversified portfolio

- Small mining companies can be very illiquid to trade in world markets

There is one more way of accessing mining stocks, and that is through Exchange Traded Funds (ETFs), which are explained in the following chapter.

## EXCHANGE-TRADED FUNDS

Exchange-Traded Funds or ETFs, are the relatively new kid on the block, combining the pooled investment potential of Unit Trusts with much lower fees. They are listed on the stock market and, as such, are tradable in the same way as ordinary shares.

From a Stocks and Shares point of view, ETFs are exciting because they can offer a much broader range of investments. Already you can invest in various hitherto unavailable indexes directly, such as Chinese or Korean stock indexes, but the great thing is that there are now even opportunities to invest in commodities such as gold and silver. This has the potential to diversify or switch your portfolio more broadly than you could ever have done so in the past.

If you have a financial advisor, then depending on the type of financial advisor you use, they may not recommend or know about ETFs simply because they do not pay enough commission. This fact alone should tell you what a comparatively good deal ETFs are.

There are two ETF types of interest to gold and silver investments, and in both cases, you can buy shares in the ETF itself through the stock market and join the party.

Some of these ETFs are simply tracking the gold or silver price. There are several gold ETFs and at least one silver ETF of this type you can invest in. You can check out ETF Securities, Blackrock's iShares, or Lyxor Gold, to name a few. Yearly fees are normally low. The funds either invest in the metals and store it in a vault or invest in the metals futures markets. Popular preference is for those funds that store the metal in a vault because your investment is more closely matched to the actual metal.

Other ETFs are simply buying a basket all of the mining stocks listed on a given stock market. These have the dual advantage of allowing investing in mining companies and achieving greater diversification than investing alone could ever do. Some of the ETFs you could consider include AMEX Gold Bugs and iShares CDN Gold, both listed in the USA.

## ADVANTAGES OF ETFS

- The costs are also much lower than comparable Unit trusts. For example, Merrill Gold Unit Trust has, at the time of writing, an initial charge of 5% and an annual charge of 1.75%. A near-equivalent ETF may have an annual charge of 0.5% and the normal costs associated with purchasing a stock on the stock market.

- For UK investors, ETFs, unlike shares, do not attract stamp duty

- Gold and silver ETFs are passive tracker investments in the main, so performance will almost match the equivalent index

- You do not have any personal storage costs to pay, and the pooled storage cost among all investors will be a lot cheaper

- For European Union investors, silver ETFs are a way of legally owning silver bullion without paying VAT

## DISADVANTAGES OF ETFS

- Smaller ETFs are very illiquid, and it can sometimes be difficult to get an on-line quote

- ETFs tend to be passive tracker investments in the main, so performance will almost match the equivalent index – yes, this was also down as an advantage, and in the main, it probably is, but some may think you can do better by direct investing in mining stocks or spread betting.

- The Metals are not physically in your possession should you need the money quickly.

Overall, ETFs definitely have a place in a diversified Metals portfolio, especially for UK investors who can invest using their tax-free ISA allowance.

## SPREAD BETTING

Here you are opening an account with a gambling website and wagering on whether the price of your chosen commodity will rise or fall in a given timescale. Bets are normally placed at a price per unit, and that price per unit is multiplied by the units you win by or lose by to calculate your profit or loss on the wager.

### ADVANTAGES OF SPREAD BETTING

- In many countries, gambling is classified as a leisure activity, and thus profits or losses are not taxable transactions. This could be a great benefit.

- There are none of the physical costs associated with ownership of the metal.

- Spread Betting could allow you to play short term movements in the metals pricing markets to your advantage. For example, you could buy and sell on the same day with low transaction costs.

## DISADVANTAGES OF SPREAD BETTING

- Your Investment is quite far removed from owning physical gold. In the event of a severe crisis where you need money on hand right now, this could be a problem.

- You need to learn about and understand the vagaries and rules of spread betting, aside from any knowledge you may have about gold or silver.

- Your bets are normally placed at a unit per point loss or profit. E.g., £5 for every cent gold falls or rises. If a bet goes against you big time, you may lose a lot more than you originally invested.

If you are still interested, then you could check out one of the many companies out there offering this service, but before you begin investing serious money in spread betting, you should find out whether it suits your style by taking advantage of one of the offers available where you test the systems by either trading for free using imaginary funds, or trading at only, say, 1 pence per point.

## THE FUTURES MARKET

Gold and silver are traded on the futures markets like any other commodity, with forward delivery dates and pricing based on what most investors expect gold to be at that time.

In case you're not sure what futures are, this is the market where a farmer or miner agrees to sell his forthcoming production at a certain price, to be delivered on a certain date. This contract can then be sold and resold by any number of investors. Whoever is holding the contract on the final delivery date is expected to take possession of the commodity in question. As an investor, you wouldn't be interested in the delivery, just trading the contract on for profit before the delivery date.

## ADVANTAGES OF THE FUTURES MARKET

- Could allow you to play short term movements in the metals pricing markets to your advantage.

- There are none of the physical costs associated with ownership of the metal.

- Many futures brokers allow you to invest "on margin," which means you can put down, say, £500 and invest up to £10,000. If a bet goes your way big time, you can make an awful lot of money.

## DISADVANTAGES OF THE FUTURES MARKET

- Your Investment is removed from owning physical gold. In the event of a severe crisis where you need money on hand right now, or the futures market closes for some reason, this could be a problem.

- You need to learn about and understand the vagaries and rules of how the futures markets work, aside from any knowledge you may have about gold or silver.

- Many futures brokers allow you to invest "on margin," which means you can put down, say, £500 and invest up to £10,000. If a bet goes against you big time, you may lose a lot more than you originally invested.

There are many companies out there offering this service.

## DERIVATIVES

Here's where you can move into really esoteric investments.

If you know a bit about the stock market, then you may have heard of things like Options or Contracts for Difference (CFDs). It is possible to play the same moves on gold and silver mining stocks or commodity prices in the same way as on other asset classes.

These are called derivatives because they are investment markets derived from the underlying asset prices, be it stock or commodity prices.

## ADVANTAGES OF DERIVATIVES

- Could allow you to play short term movements in the metals pricing markets to your advantage.

- There are none of the physical costs associated with ownership of the metal.

- Options and derivatives are a geared play on an asset class movement. A small price movement in your favour can multiply the value of your original investment many times over.

## DISADVANTAGES OF DERIVATIVES

- Your Investment is removed from owning physical gold. In the event of a severe crisis where you need money on hand right now, or the market closes for some reason, this could be a problem.

- You need to learn about and understand the vagaries and rules of how the markets work, aside from any knowledge you may have about gold or silver.

- Options and derivatives are normally geared play on an asset class movement. Even a small move against you can destroy your original investment and leave you owing a lot more besides.

To summarise, derivatives may not be the best investing move for the introductory gold and silver investors this book is intended for. They require a lot of specialist knowledge, and if you really want to find out more about options trading and other related investment classes, then it is recommended that you read specialist literature and become comfortable with the concepts before risking any of your investment capital.

## PERTH MINT CERTIFICATES

Perth Mint certificates are a way of buying title to Australian gold through certificates. The Perth Mint has existed since 1899 and is backed by the State government of Western Australia.

They offer both Allocated and Unallocated storage. These two options were described in the section on gold Storage, and you may remember that Allocated is the recommended option. Allocated attracts a fabrication and storage fee in this case, but unallocated does not.

These can only be bought through official brokers of Perth Mint certificates. The research suggested that they do not all charge the same fees, so it is recommended you visit the list of recommended brokers on their website and investigate thoroughly. For example, *Pacific Capital* quoted a lesser price than *Gold and Silver Investments*, even though the latter was a more local dealer for the author (UK and Ireland). You should be able to use any dealer you wish.

There are many ID requirements for people wishing to invest in Perth Mint Certificates, including a potential need for notarised documents from a lawyer, so this might be something else you need to consider in your investing plans.

### ADVANTAGES OF PERTH MINT CERTIFICATES

- Western Government-backed guarantee

- For the likes of the US or European investors, for example, your Investment lies far away from local government jurisdiction

- Low Fees

- Offers allocated storage

- No VAT on silver purchases for EU buyers

## DISADVANTAGES OF PERTH MINT CERTIFICATES

- High initial investment required (10,000 US$)

- Can only cash in the bonds in large units

- Only a limited number of brokers retail this service

- The service is paper-based and not internet-based, so it may take a while to get your money back when you decide to cash in, and, unless you live in Perth, your metals could be very hard to access in a time of crisis

The conclusion is that those looking to squirrel away a large sum for long-term investment purposes may find these the best investing option. Their Australian location may also appeal to those subject to other government jurisdictions. The Perth Mint does, in fact, advertise that no taxes are payable on purchases or sales of precious metals in Australia and that Australia allows free movement of precious metals in and out of Australia.

## ELECTRONIC GOLD AND SILVER

Electronic gold, and more lately, electronic silver, is a superb idea that could only ever have been made possible by the internet. The theory is that you exchange your money with an internet-based organisation that gives you an account containing an equivalent number of gold units. These gold units are your bank account and theoretically backed by an equivalent amount of gold held on storage somewhere.

The gold units you hold can be held or exchanged for services bought over the internet. If you hold the units, you will have to pay a storage fee for your gold, although as with ETFs, this will be less than trying to go it alone. Normally, storage will also be *Allocated*, and you might remember that this is the preferred storage option, since it means there is some real metal out there that belongs to you.

You are normally free to exchange your gold back into a variety of national currencies at any time, at the prevailing gold exchange rate less a small fee, either fixed or a percentage. Some providers allow you to retain your national currency with them; others will pay it back to you. The ease with which you can withdraw your currency and receive it back in your bank account is also something you may need to consider.

The Major Fees to Consider are:-

<u>Storage Cost</u>

Usually quoted monthly as a percentage or a fixed amount. The fixed amount is normally the best deal for larger holdings.

<u>Buy Transaction Cost</u>

Same as with coins, there will be a bid-offer spread, where you pay, say, 2% over the spot price to buy. Also, remember to investigate whether there will be any other fees applicable to your situation, for example, personal bank fees if you live in Norway and the digital currency provider only accepts dollars.

<u>Sell Transaction Cost</u>

Just the same as with coins, there will be a bid-offer spread where you receive, say, 2% under spot price when you sell. Also, remember to investigate whether there will be any other fees applicable to your situation, for example, money transfer fees if you need your money in Norwegian Krone, and the e-gold provider only pays out dollars.

<u>Possibilities for use as a digital currency</u>

Would you like to spend your gold directly on other products instead of exchanging them into national currency? If so, then this could be useful, as more and more internet retailers are offering this as an option. Remember to investigate whether the fees are suited to the type of transactions you think you'll be making.

## ADVANTAGES OF ELECTRONIC GOLD AND SILVER

- Internet-based, so a very accessible product with low costs

- Pooled investment, so secure storage costs are less than going it alone

- Your investment can be stored safely outside of local government jurisdiction

- Easy to buy and sell just by logging in to your PC

- Can be used as a medium of exchange in business transactions, and can even work out cheaper than bank conversion of national currencies

## DISADVANTAGES OF ELECTRONIC GOLD AND SILVER

- You are trusting a third party organisation with your wealth, so you need to be sure that they are definitely holding the relevant amount of gold to meet all their depositors. If a particular organisation ever gets into trouble, your gold and entire wealth could be at risk.

- Governments may target digital currency providers because they feel they are missing out on tax revenue or that their National currencies are being undermined. Ironically, the USA, long-regarded as the "land of the free," is currently leading the way in this respect. How this affects your savings is uncertain.

- Unlike credit card payments, payments with digital currency are usually irreversible. Most providers do make this major difference clear upfront, so if there are any issues concerning a transaction, E.g. faulty or non-delivered goods, then it would be up to you to chase up the situation with whatever legal backing is necessary. eBay banned the use of E-Gold and used to cancel any auction offering E-Gold as a payment method. However, some critics claimed that this is mainly done to protect their vested interest in PayPal, at that time their own online payments system.

Before going any further, some readers may ask why electronic currency providers, unlike banks and bank deposits, aren't regulated or financially backed by the government in any way has not been listed as a major disadvantage. Well, to be honest, part of the attraction of gold is the independence of national borders and constraints that holding it should bring. Considering past histories of government mismanagement of national currencies and the confiscation of wealth, who can you really truly trust to look after your hard-earned money?

The major people involved with the well-known digital currency businesses are all greatly enthusiastic about the subject of gold, 100% believe in gold as the one true store of value and often write articles displaying their depth of knowledge on the subject. So when it comes to trust, could you really consider them to be any less trustworthy than the average politician and the unaudited gold reserves your nation-state claims to hold?

There are many providers out there, but as a British citizen living in the European Union, many of them were found to be heavily slanted towards the US market. For example, only accepting payment in dollars or paying out in dollars.

One more thing you will have to consider is the application criteria for your chosen provider. In order to meet with government money laundering regulations and the like, many providers require multiple copies of documents for proof of you and your address, and perhaps even notarised documents from your bank or lawyer. This can add extra administration, cost, and time to opening an account.

We'll now cover some of the main providers that cater or catered for citizens throughout the world. Not discriminating against non-US citizens, by which it is meant non-US citizens who otherwise might end up paying extra bank transfer fees, etc.

## E-GOLD

E-Gold was one of the first organisations to offer this service. It has also become, like Liberty Dollar, an example of the reach of the USA in suppressing threats to its financial prominence in the current imperial era. Back in 2007, "How to Invest in Gold and Silver" suggested it as a possible internet gold solution but stated that their links with usage for illegal payments could count against them. So it proved. Whether or not E-gold itself was to blame, the USA went for it with gusto, confiscating the gold and closing it down.

It was started up by a Dr Jackson, who strongly believed in the gold story, and that gold was due to make a comeback as the trusted medium of exchange. On that score, he was right. E-gold started out in the USA and then moved their jurisdiction to Nevis in the West Indies. Even not being based on US soil wasn't enough to save them, which suggests the reach of an Empire when it sees competitors.

They offered deposit facilities and also heavily promoted the use of e-gold for payments. There could have been an exciting future for e-gold, but unfortunately, they had to deal with various allegations made by the US Government, including aiding and abetting illegal activity and running an unregistered banking institution.

Some critics even now wonder whether the reason they were being chased is the alleged use of e-Gold for fraudulent purposes, or whether it was an attempt to stop US citizens from dumping the ailing dollar, placing their wealth outside of US jurisdiction, and using a truly international hard currency. E-Gold had such success with gold that they even offered e-Silver, e-Platinum, and e-Palladium too.

Considering what happened to e-Gold and Liberty Dollar, any US citizen should probably be monitoring the actions of their government very carefully right now, as they seem to be curtailing a lot of the principles attached to the free movement of wealth, internet gambling being another example. As fair or unfair as this ongoing saga may be, if you are a US citizen, you might want to consider your own intended usage of any digital currency provider because of government actions. Nobody can possibly predict future legislation and its effect on business dealings, least of all this book.

## GOLDMONEY

This was the brainchild of highly-respected gold watcher James Turk. Goldmoney was structured with a cast-iron guarantee that there will always be 100% gold backing of every unit of currency (called "goldgrams" in this case) in circulation, and they claim that some others do not have the same cast-iron guarantees in their small print. Whether this is true or not is hard to say, as for an ordinary investor, the small-print is difficult to understand, but the discussions and articles available make interesting reading when deciding on the safety of providers you are considering.

Goldmoney, like e-Gold did, also tries to offer the use of Goldmoney as a medium of payment. This, however, is not very heavily used right now, and the majority of investors are gold bugs simply buying gold and silver and holding it.

What could appeal to British or EU citizens about Goldmoney is that it is Jersey-based. You may trust and understand the rules of Jersey more than those of the Caribbean or Panama. This is not to say that other organisations are unsafe. A US-citizen may just as easily understand Panama and believe it to be much safer than Jersey.

As time went by, Goldmoney has opened a variety of vaults to cater for the requirements of international buyers, including London, New York, Zurich, Singapore, and Hong Kong.

GoldMoney also has a silver option, and this represents an excellent opportunity for European Union buyers to buy silver bullion without legally paying any VAT. More latterly, they also introduced the ability to hold the national currencies of Dollars, Pounds, or Euros in your Goldmoney account and receive interest on it. You can then switch your holding between any of the five denominations (including the two metals), as you see fit.

Knowing that it's the fees that make investors poor and brokers rich, you are probably best off not utilising this feature. The fees will quickly eat into your returns, and a buy-and-hold strategy is probably best.

Payment into GoldMoney is by bank transfer. Payment out can be made by direct bank transfer.

One other aspect of GoldMoney worthy of mention is that at one point, the terms and conditions said that if your account is not logged into for 12 years, the ownership of your gold reverted to Goldmoney. Okay, it sounds unlikely, but consider what would happen if you died and never told anybody about your holding or even if you could not use the internet for 12 years due to some kind of accident or national crisis.

Overall, a highly respected organisation with the reputation of a known "gold-watcher" behind it. Even if you don't buy Goldmoney, then there are articles available for free on the website that make interesting reading.

## BULLIONVAULT

Founded by Paul Tustain, BullionVault sits somewhere between Goldmoney, for safety and Gold storage, and the trading services mentioned earlier. Bullionvault is UK-based, although an additional interesting feature is the ability to store your gold in their New York, London, or Zurich gold vaults. Dependent on which country you are a citizen of, you will probably feel most comfortable placing your gold outside of that country, so that is not subject to your local government jurisdiction, so top marks for considering that feature.

An interesting aspect of the three separate vaults is that these could be considered as separate currencies in their own right. For example, if at some point in the future there was a repeat of the 1930s US Gold confiscation, gold stored in a New York Vault might become priced significantly lower than gold stored in a Zurich vault, as US holders try to sell and place their gold outside their own jurisdiction.

BullionVault allows you to buy and sell Gold on their impressive-looking trading platform, where buyers and sellers of gold from each vault can meet and state their required selling/buying prices, so if you are more inclined to hold gold, occasionally sell on a dip, then buy in again later, then this could well be the best service for you.

Their fees for transactions and monthly storage are really low, too, so they are very worthy of investigation. The storage fee is currently $4.46 per month fixed, regardless of holding size, and only payable for the months in which you held Gold.

Again, Bullionvault has proved popular with Gold Bugs accumulating gold for the future financial crisis they believe is in the offing.

Payment into BullionVault is by bank transfer. Payment out is by bank wire transfer to your chosen bank account.

In recent years, they introduced a silver option. That they took so long may have been something to do with BullionVault being UK-based and the UK charging VAT on silver sales, which could, to many observers, seem to be another example of government getting in the way of free trade.

## GOLD AND SILVER INVESTING SCAMS

It would be unwise to complete this book without warning you about some of the major scams being perpetrated today. The sad thing is that many of these scams use the worldwide reputation of value and wealth that precious metals, especially gold, represent as a way to lure naïve investors into parting with their cash.

Firstly, never buy gold of uncertain value from unknown sources. This could include jewellery from street traders or even coins from internet auction sellers with no prior sales record. There is simply too much at risk to do otherwise unless you feel that the lower price you are paying justifies the risk. In most, if not all cases, it will not, so when buying physical gold, always buy from reputable, well-established sources with good feedback.

Secondly, if a deal looks too good to be true, it probably is. The price of gold in various currencies is listed everywhere daily, so anyone with gold knows its approximate value, therefore why would they offer to sell it to you cheaply? Often people believe they have bought gold bars, later to find that they are lead inside, as lead is a similar weight. Again, to be safe here, only consider buying only from reputable sources where you can go for redress if anything goes wrong.

The internet, abounding with opportunities, whilst also fraught with dangers, is the new wild west of the 21st century, and has also brought forth new avenues for criminals. One of the most common of these is a *Gold Investing scam*. These scammers play on people having heard about digital precious metal-backed currencies, but not knowing how they work. Many of these scammers can be found advertising on the right-hand side of the Google search engine in the Google-Ads section if you make a gold-related search, making outlandish claims such as "make ½ to 5% per day" or "double your money in 30 days". If you are happy that your PC is protected against things like viruses and other worm software infecting it, then you could try visiting some of these sites to familiarise yourself with the type of cons being perpetrated. Furthermore, every click from Google costs these scammers money, which can be no bad thing either. Google is blameless here, as their Adwords is an excellent service for legitimate businesses and individuals to reach their target audience, and there is no way they could be considered accountable for the actions of a criminal minority.

After clicking on the ad, what you'll often then find is a credible-looking website, with heavy use of financial terms and acronyms such as HYIP (High Yield Investment Program), that doesn't really mean much, along with outlandish claims about how you will get rich by starting with a small sum, like, say $50. This is often backed up by some unintelligible diagram showing gold being routed between various parties and somehow ending up in your account. Even after reading it carefully, you usually still don't understand how the money is made, and searching around the site for real contact details such as a name, address, or telephone number throw up very little if anything relevant.

Please don't ever be conned by these websites or even dubious emails, often from places like Nigeria, offering you the chance to make instant, huge sums of money through gold, silver, digital currency, or whatever. If it looks too good to be true, and you can't understand how it works, then it is most probably best to avoid it.

The truth is, if anyone can truly find an investment that returns even ½% per day, the best approach would be to keep quiet until you owned all the gold in the entire world, which, with compounding, actually probably wouldn't take as long as you think!

There are plenty of sites out there full of sad cases of people sharing with others their experiences of how their money has gone, with no replies and no money back. Given the fact that very few of us, if any, ever get the right financial training in our early years, including schooling, to prepare us for the serious financial decisions we'll have to make in our adult lives, is it a wonder so many naïve and trusting people can be conned by such schemes?

The overriding advice here is to only invest with reputable and well-established gold sites.

## INTERNET AUCTION SITE SCAMS

While Internet auction sites are a highly recommended resource for buying many things, precious metals, especially gold, are probably not among them.

When you are trading something like gold, it is important to know you are buying from a reputable source, with a comeback, if anything is wrong with your purchase. Aside from this, you also have to consider postal costs and possible import duties on top.

If you ever do find yourself buying something from the likes of eBay, then follow a few simple guidelines. Make sure you pay using PayPal, and that your account is funded using a credit card. This gives you the most protection to get your money back if anything goes wrong with the transaction, such as the goods not turning up or being not as described.

Another scam to be aware of is when selling items of your own on eBay. eBay is mentioned here specifically, not because eBay is in any way a fraudulent site, but mainly because of its major associations with its payment processing company, PayPal and the lack of understanding of how it works by sellers. Often buyers from strange countries far from your own will bid on your items and pay using PayPal. After a few weeks, they will register the non-arrival of your item, even though you know you sent it, and it most probably arrived fine. Under such circumstances, they will claim for, and eventually receive a refund from PayPal, and PayPal will then take the money back from you. Unless you took out adequate insurance on the item, which the buyer should pay for, and successfully claim for your loss from the Post Office, then you are the loser. You are warned about this to make a clear decision about offering PayPal as a payment option when selling valuable items such as gold coins.

## SUMMARY

Traditionally, holding gold meant either gold coins or jewellery, stored either in your home or local bank, but the internet and electronic trading platforms on it have opened up a new world of gold and silver investing to the normal man on the street.

Many previously closed ways of investing in gold easily, such as share-dealing or futures trading, are now available, but it has also spawned spread betting and the completely new concept of *digital currency.*

In the case of digital currency, the declining value of national currencies and rising worldwide internet access could see this new medium for storing wealth and facilitating trade come to the fore, and we may yet only be in the early days of a new monetary paradigm.

Armed with the knowledge that these options are available, you should feel confident about investing in gold and silver in the ways that best suit your needs and at the lowest fees.

And now it's time to reiterate that this publication is not directly inducing you to invest or not invest in any particular product, merely to identify opportunities to invest more cheaply, so that more of your money remains your own and secondly to identify possible areas of precious metals investment that are unknown to the majority of investors yet offer great scope to diversify your portfolio and improve your returns.

Please remember to visit the website to check out all of the links in this publication and also find recommended reading at:- http://www.investgold.co.uk

Made in the USA
Monee, IL
07 July 2026